ESSENTIAL
WOODCARVING
TECHNIQUES

ESSENTIAL WOODCARVING TECHNIQUES

Dick Onians

GUILD OF MASTER CRAFTSMAN PUBLICATIONS LTD

First published 1997 by
Guild of Master Craftsman Publications Ltd
166 High Street · Lewes · East Sussex · BN7 1XU

Reprinted 1997

Photography by Richard Lathbury Onians
Line drawings by John Yates

ISBN 1 86108 042 5

Designed by Lovelock & Co

Set in Adobe Garamond

Printed and bound in Singapore under the supervision of MRM Graphics,
Winslow, Buckinghamshire, UK

MEASUREMENTS

Although care has been taken to ensure that imperial measurements are true
and accurate, they are only conversions from metric. Throughout the book
instances may be found where a metric measurement has slightly varying
imperial equivalents, because in each particular case the closest imperial
equivalent has been given. Care should be taken to use either imperial or
metric measurements consistently. Some discrepancies arise where sizes of
equipment made to one system of measurement do not correspond exactly
to that in the other. Other discrepancies merely indicate that small variations
in sizes quoted are not critical to the success of a carving.

This book is dedicated to the memory of William Wheeler
who taught me, and to the memory of my father
and to my mother who encouraged me

CONTENTS

ACKNOWLEDGEMENTS

I should like to thank my many past and present students, friends and colleagues who have encouraged me and who have knowingly and unknowingly contributed material for the photographs. Particular thanks are due to Hugh Annesley, Norman Barback, Susan Harrison, Lisa Higgo, Jamie McCarthy, Janet Monks, Percival Morgan and Leslie Pollard for allowing carving in progress and finished work to be photographed when they knew I might criticize it. Howard Spiers has been especially generous in this. As far as possible I have attributed work photographed to its maker. I should also like to thank Gillian Maddison for her great help with the chapter on lettering and Philip Surey for drawing the sample alphabet. My gratitude also goes to Leslie Lonsdale-Cooper who put the idea of this book in my mind years ago, encouraged me and unstintingly gave both time and advice about the writing. I should also like to thank the staff of GMC Publications for their patience, help and unfailing courtesy. Finally, I am most grateful to my wife Frances, not only for putting up with the writing for three years and for typing most of it for me, but also for her unflagging good humour and support.

INTRODUCTION

Largely inactive since the 1940s, the woodcarving genius of Britain and the English-speaking world is reviving after a period when the tradition was shrunk by apathy, lack of demand and increasing mechanization. Now, perhaps as a revulsion against the lifelessness of machine-made objects and certainly as a response to greater leisure and longer retirement, an increasing number of classes are offered, and in their wake new books and magazine articles proliferate. It is, however, very much an amateur revival; the old craftsmen are few and not all are willing or able to teach. Tastes, too, have changed, and new machines and tools are becoming necessary parts of the professional workshop; they remove drudgery and they are convenient and faster.

Twenty-eight years of teaching traditional and modern woodcarving has taught me two things. Firstly, if left to explore the tools for themselves, students limit their style and subjects and develop technique very slowly or not at all. Secondly, they intend to do carving, so carving is what they do. They may be persuaded to draw what they are going to carve or to make a model, but for most the design is something to be worked out on the carving in progress. Rather than train their powers of observation, develop a sense of sculptural form

and learn a repertoire of natural and conventional forms, many rely on the knowledge, skill and time of the tutor. An important theme of this book is the encouragement of carvers to overcome their diffidence about their drawing and artistic ability.

To meet this deficiency I prepared a course with a regular progression through techniques for the City and Guilds of London Institute's Creative Studies series. The present book closely follows this progression. It is designed to cover the technical aspects that a carver should master before he or she is competent, and because some carvers are interested in traditional and others in more creative carving I have covered both in this book. The projects are arranged so that techniques of carving and ways of thinking build on those before. The City and Guilds Creative Studies courses are accompanied by a compulsory course in Preparing Working Designs. Design and drawing ability are best learned by attending classes, but I have indicated some of the problems and have suggested how they may be overcome.

Space, however, limits the range of techniques covered, including some advanced subjects – for example, relief carving of scenes and people has been omitted. Although it is popular with beginners it is a special discipline, demanding not only good draughtsmanship but also much practice with perspective and the foreshortening of forms that are difficult to carve in the round.

Woodcarving covers many different techniques and tools, but here I concentrate on carving with chisels. Chain saws, angle grinders and other machines are referred to as useful aids, particularly when roughing out a carving, but the greatest skill and sense of achievement comes from carving with chisels.

Writing a book to teach practical techniques is risky. The best way to learn carving is by watching it being demonstrated and then practising under the eye of a constructively critical teacher. This book is therefore intended only as a guide, and it will be seen that for all but the first two projects – chip carving and the carving of mouldings – design is your responsibility. Examples are given to illustrate principles; they are not intended as patterns for you to follow (although of course you may do so, except in the case of recent original works which are covered by copyright). Even if the resulting designs are not works of great art they will be your own and therefore be much more fulfilling to carve.

Bad examples are shown as well as good in order to illustrate common faults and how they can be avoided. I particularly stress the need for preparation, not only by study of the subjects to be carved but also by planning the designs and ways of holding the wood.

As is said in military circles, time spent on reconnaissance is seldom wasted. This is more true in carving than in other forms of art where it is comparatively easy to rectify a mistake. Furthermore, when the form has been truly considered and learnt, the carving goes so much more confidently. The wood responds more willingly to the chisel; there is less stopping to decide what to do next. The result is a fluent and lively piece of work. Of course, mistakes do

happen, and the wood does not always behave as expected. If you have a good idea of what you are making you may adapt the mistake to your advantage. What we forget when looking at carvings made by others is that things probably went wrong at some stage for their makers but they were able to change their plans. I often feel that it is at this point that a work becomes alive. We tend to force things into a symmetry which can be lifeless. I refer in Chapters 5 and 6 to the difference between Victorian and medieval Gothic carvings to make this point. The same problem can arise if one works very closely with a clay model or an original carving. Unless you are asked for an exact replica you should allow something of yourself into the carving, for then it comes alive. The more experience and technique you have at your disposal, the more you know that it is yourself that you are putting into it, and not just a series of happy (or unhappy) accidents.

Taste is inevitably subjective, but it develops through exposure to many examples of good work. Study of old and modern masters' woodcarvings and sculptures in other materials should help you to see why, for instance, I recommend certain ways of finishing carvings.

Carving is a form of sculpture. When you copy a natural form in wood it cannot be the same as the original. If you copy a leaf it cannot be literally as thin as a leaf. If you succeed in making one so thin, it will soon be broken and will merely demonstrate your patience and not your judgement. Likewise, you cannot reproduce exactly every pore or vein or hair. It is worth seeing how earlier carvers created the illusion of reality or worked from nature to invent their own forms.

Many carvers since Victorian times have been women. I trust that I shall be excused if I avoid the clumsy 'he or she' in the text and follow tradition by using 'he' throughout.

A novice sometimes embarks on an over-ambitious project which takes far longer than it would have done if he had left it until he had more experience. The result is often either a botched job or frustration, or both. By first patiently developing skill on simpler tasks he could have made several other carvings as well as this one in the same time. Abstract sculpture also offers pitfalls. One may succeed by beginner's luck but this is unusual and unlikely to last. It is easy to make an abstract, but very difficult to make a good one. This book contains advice on stylization of natural and man-made objects, showing how abstract sculptures may be inspired by them, as well as on making purely abstract shapes.

Much modern teaching of art rejects the copying of earlier work as a practice likely to stifle self-expression and original creativity. It also appears to disapprove of the learning of techniques since, in the past, they sometimes became ends in themselves and made for sterile work. There is truth in this, but it is equally true that, since what we now call art began, man has continually overcome design and technical problems. I believe it is folly, if not arrogance, to dismiss what our predecessors discovered. Technique, too, is like language. Without a language which is spoken and understood by others, our thoughts are liable at best to misinterpretation, at worst to complete incomprehension. If artists and craftspeople feel the need to create simply for themselves it is possible that the absence of technique poses no problem to them, but once they have decided to display their work to others there is an evident attempt at communication. The work may contain different levels of meaning, but I believe that it should reach the viewer on at least one level.

There is a story attributed to Picasso that, after hearing a headmistress gushing over the primitive innocence of her pupils' art, he remarked that when he was twelve he could draw like Michelangelo. The message here is reassuring to those who fear for the safety of their own creativity. Simply copying what others have done is stultifying if not accompanied by that training of the powers of observation and individual expression which the practice both of drawing and modelling from life and nature and of designing gives.

When I began to teach carving in recreational classes I quickly learnt that a good way to lose students was to start with chisel-sharpening. Unless they were committed to a long, serious course, I found it best to let students discover the problems and pleasures of using blunt and sharp tools first. You may wish to follow this example and skip the section in Chapter 1 on chisel-sharpening until you feel the need. It will mean more to you then. Indeed, Chapters 1 and 2 may mean more to you when you have read the rest. Apart from sharpening, the essential equipment and woods are described where relevant in subsequent chapters.

I do not claim that the techniques I describe in this book are the only ways of doing things. The late William Wheeler used to tell how he had been taught by three part-time tutors on successive days. Every day a tutor told him how to do the work, but the following day the next tutor asked him what fool had told him to tackle his sculpture like that and then declared, 'Now this is how you do it.' Eventually he got them together and told them that as he was being taught by three fools he would listen to what each said, then do what seemed right to him. After all, the only right way to do anything is the way that works for you.

The best way to learn carving is with an intelligent and experienced carver. Nevertheless, I hope that this book will give serious students a sound background of carving skills and confidence in design.

CHAPTER 1

TOOLS AND EQUIPMENT

The Differences between Carving and Carpentry Chisels

In the European tradition, carving has been done with a variety of tools associated with other professions: axes, adzes and spokeshaves, the tools of the forester and carpenter and of specialized trades such as the hurdle-maker and the wheelwright. Smaller work done with a knife, known as whittling, must be among the most ancient of forms, but the tools of the carpenter, especially chisels, have always been most used.

Although the word 'chisels' is used specifically of straight-edged tools, it also embraces **gouges** and **V tools.** Beginners, having nothing to compare them with, often start with poor or inappropriate chisels and blame themselves for their slow progress or rough finish. Some despair and give up. While it is possible to achieve some sort of result with carpentry chisels and with the clumsy carving chisels produced by some manufacturers,

it makes more sense to use good tools. If you are satisfied with a crude finish and do not mind how long the work takes, this is not important. But it *is* important if you want to get the best out of the tools and work smoothly and efficiently.

There are about five main differences between good carving chisels and carpentry chisels. The carpenter and joiner need robust chisels. Much of the work done with a carpenter's chisel is hidden inside joints or carcassing and so, although sharpness makes the work easier, a blunt tool will not ruin the work. Because a carver uses chisels almost exclusively, a blunt tool not only leaves torn fibres but also slows the work. Consequently there is likely to be a marked difference in the quality of the steel used and in the thickness of the blade.

A carver needs a tool which will hold a good edge when driven with a mallet, yet be light enough for paring. If the metal is thick, much grinding is needed to get a thin enough edge. Very thick blades may be made of poor steel, or in

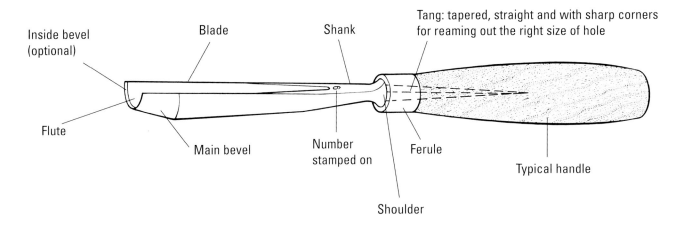

FIG 1.1 *The parts of a chisel.*

ignorance of a carver's needs. The extra thickness would be needed to give the strength to resist the shocks and leverage demanded by carving only if the metal were poor. If one looks at the best modern tools but, more particularly, at chisels made before 1940, it is clear that such thickness is not necessary.

Carpentry and joinery tools look as if they have been stamped out and their shanks have been filed or turned very regularly. The sides of the blades are cut square and usually the metal is the same thickness from one side of the blade to the other. Carving chisels, on the other hand, may be of uneven thickness and be rounded up to the sides to make them thinner. Their **shanks** taper down to the **shoulders** where they meet the handles. The other main difference is that carving chisels made since the beginning of the twentieth century have numbers stamped on them to indicate the shape of the tool (Fig 1.1). Regrettably, some modern manufacturers omit this altogether, or put the number impermanently on the handle. Sometimes, even, the wrong numbers are stamped.

Handles may be a guide, since carpenters' and joiners' tools tend to have waists. Carvers' chisels may have square, octagonal or tapered cylindrical handles. Some carvers vary the woods and shapes of handles to make for easy recognition.

Because a carver works almost exclusively with chisels, their shapes and sizes have been varied to cope with particular problems and to speed the work. In the past carvers either forged their own tools, or designed them for particular purposes and had them made. Nowadays the range is enormous, although with the decline in traditional carving some manufacturers no longer make them all and others will only make very specialized ones on request.

THE COMMONEST SHAPES OF CARVING CHISELS AND THEIR NUMBERING

There are 14 main end-of-blade shapes to chisels, and in the English (Sheffield) system they are numbered 1 to 11 and 39, 41 and 45. Other countries use slightly different numbers, but they all seem to agree that the lowest number indicates a flat or straight-edged chisel.

In the Sheffield system a chisel with a straight edge at right angles to the axis of the blade is a

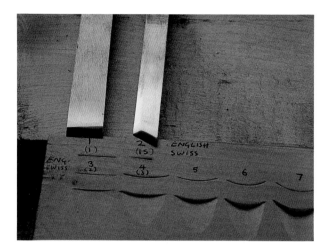

FIG 1.2 *No. 1 straight-edge and No. 2 skew chisel. Note that the metal has been ground back on the side running from the obtuse angle to make it less likely to pinch in a groove.*

FIG 1.3 *Long bend and short front-bend (or bent) or spoon bit gouges.*

No. 1 (Fig 1.2). If the straight edge is at an angle to the axis it is a No. 2 **corner** or **skew** chisel. Both are usually bevelled on each side. The others up to No. 11 are gouges, starting with the No. 3 **extra-flat** gouge. At first glance this looks like a **straight-edge**, a misreading which has led to many of these useful tools being ground flat on both sides. It is in fact slightly curved. The depth of the curve or **sweep** increases with each number until No. 11, which is approximately U-shaped. The next numbers in the English system are the **long** or **salmon bend** and the **short front-bent** or **spoon bit** chisels (Fig 1.3). These start with the conventional straight-edge (No. 21), and both left- and right-handed bent skew chisels are made so that corners may be approached from any direction. Numbers 22 and 23 (Fig 1.4) are both skews, and the extra flat gouge is No. 24.

The sweeps progress in the usual way up to 32 (equivalent to that of a straight No. 11 gouge). From 33 to 38 the tools look like upside-down spoon bit gouges. These are **backbent** gouges (Fig 1.5). The next numbers are **V** or **parting tools** of 45°, 60° and 90°. The **macaroni,**

fluteroni, **backeroni** and **wing parting tools** (Fig 1.6) are very rarely used now except by specialist trade carvers and restorers. Most of the Nos. 1–11 are made in **fishtail** or in **long pod** versions. A good fishtail chisel has an angle of about 60° at each corner. It may also be called a **spade tool**. The long pod chisel has a less sharp angle at each corner and a longer splay. A common mistake with fishtail and other tapered tools is to round the ends (Fig 1.7). While this might produce a shape that is useful for certain jobs it is a waste of a good and extremely useful tapered tool. The fishtail's corners are thin and so reach better into corners (Fig 1.8).

Some chisels are tapered from the shoulder to the edge, which gives a compromise between the strength of a straight tool and the ability of a spade tool to cut cleanly into corners.

CHOOSING YOUR FIRST SHAPES AND SIZES OF CHISEL

Out of all these chisels, where do you start when you begin to collect them for your own work?

FIG 1.4 *Left- and right-hand skew front bent chisels, Nos 22 and 23. Square-ended ones can be modified to produce the same shapes.*

FIG 1.5 *Backbent.*

FIG 1.6 *Clockwise from top left: wing parting-tool, macaroni, backbent fluteroni, Cogelow left- and right-handed skew gouges and at the bottom a V chisel with a prong at the tip, and one with a skewed end or reverse rake.*

FIG 1.7 *Fishtails – from top: Swiss No. 3, English No. 3 and No. 5. Note the greater splay on the English tools and the rounded end of the No. 5 which reduces the tool's usefulness.*

Contrary to what some manufacturers tell us, there is no such thing as a beginner's set. What you want depends entirely on what you are going to carve and its size. Besides, sets often seem to contain at least one tool that is never used.

My advice is to borrow tools from someone's teaching set – most carvers are jealous of their own tools – and see which ones you use most before you buy. With experience, particularly if you have been taught how to carve traditional foliage and chip carving, you can predict which tools you will need.

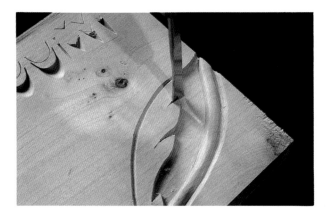

FIG 1.8 *Fishtail being used to stab into a corner.*

CHOOSING THE MAKES OF TOOL

Again, I recommend that you are careful about which make of chisel you buy, as unfortunately some are not as good as you might expect. Ask professionals who have had experience of many makes which are safe to buy. If I were to put modern manufacturers in my own order of preference I should regretfully give first place to some foreign makers.

Factors to consider are edge-holding ability, strength combined with slenderness (and consistency of these factors in all tools of the same make), competitive price, width of range and availability. Some tools are sold already sharpened. Some makes are always sold with their backs polished, a largely cosmetic exercise. Some are available without handles, which gives the new owner the chance to make his tools quickly recognizable.

My own list (overleaf) is not exhaustive, but is based on my own experience and that of students and colleagues over many years. Some foreign makes I have used only occasionally.

Japanese chisels have an excellent reputation for holding a sharp edge. However, the way they are made means that the **bevel** must be steep, which makes long cuts difficult. The Japanese style of

carving is to use short, scooping cuts. These chisels are expensive.

It is a mistake to think that it is sensible to start with cheap tools (not that price always equals quality). Tools which are clumsy, impossible to bring to a sharp edge or will not hold an edge cause many beginners to become frustrated or lose confidence.

BUYING OLD TOOLS

Tools made before 1940 are generally safe except for ones which look very short – they may have been favourite tools, but they are more likely to have been endlessly sharpened because they were poor. Rust is best avoided unless you know what you are looking at. Rust on the inside of the **flute** of a gouge is only acceptable if you are confident it will be cut through to bright metal with an inside bevel, something which is best avoided on bent and V chisels. Rust on the underside is easier to cope with. Bad pitting on the inside, or on the side or near the handle, weakens a tool and may make it worthless. The best-known second-hand makes are Addis and Herring Bros. Earlier tools can sometimes be dated. If a tool has 'Prize medals 51' stamped on it, it was made between the exhibitions of 1851 and 1862. Earlier tools have only the makers' names. Tools made before 1900 seldom have their sweep numbers stamped on them. Some old tools were home-made and are not name-stamped, and you take your chance with them. Unfortunately, collectors who only want old tools for display have pushed up the price. Incidentally there are new tools with the name Addis on a label on the handle, but I have not yet used them and so must reserve judgement.

When buying unhandled chisels ensure that the shape and alignment of the **tang** are true (*see* Fig 1.1). The tang should be straight in line with the blade. It should be of square section, with sharp edges. Unless you have drill bits of exactly the

		MAKES OF TOOL		
Maker/brand	**Country**	**Edge-holding**	**Slenderness**	
Pfeil	Switzerland	Consistently good	Good	
Stubai	Austria	Consistently good	Good	
Carl Heidtmann	Germany	Consistently good	Good	
Mifer	Spain	Good but brittle	Variable	
Auriou	France	Consistently good	Good	
Bristol Design	Britain	Consistently good	Good	
Robert Sorby	Britain	Consistently good	Narrow tools too thick	
Ashley Iles	Britain	Consistently soft but good	Variable	
Henry Taylor (Acorn brand)	Britain	Inconsistent, some are very good	Variable	
Marples	Britain	Occasionally good	Generally thick	
Maker/brand	**Price**	**Width of range**	**Availability**	
Pfeil	Moderately expensive, can vary	Fairly wide	Full range from few suppliers	
Stubai	Moderately expensive	Wide	Only in Austria	
Carl Heidtmann	Moderate	Wide	Only in Germany	
Mifer	Not known	Fairly wide	Not known	
Auriou	High	Wide	One British supplier	
Bristol Design	High	Fairly wide	Bristol Design only	
Robert Sorby	Moderate	Fairly limited	Selected outlets	
Ashley Iles	Moderate	Wide	Selected outlets	
Henry Taylor	Moderate	Virtually complete	Many suppliers (few sell a wide range)	
Marples	Moderate	Fairly wide	Easily found, usually in sets	

right sizes and can drill the holes in the handles accurately, make sure that the tang is tapered to a point. The best way to fit a handle is to fix the chisel in a vice and then gently tap the handle on to the tang, rotating the handle and frequently shaking out the wood that the corners of the tang ream out. When the shoulder of the chisel is about 6mm (¼in) from the handle make sure that the blade is in line with the handle. It may need to be rotated for this. It is particularly important that the blade does not veer to one side. If you have to choose between anhedral (pointing downwards) and dihedral (pointing upwards), choose dihedral. A handle of a hard wood such as box needs to be closer to the shoulder before being driven home. The handle is driven on with a strong mallet stroke.

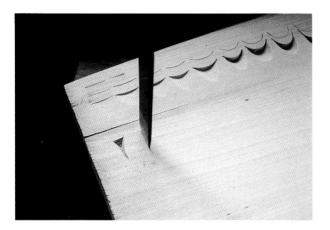

FIG 1.9 *No. 1 straight-edge stabbing a straight line.*

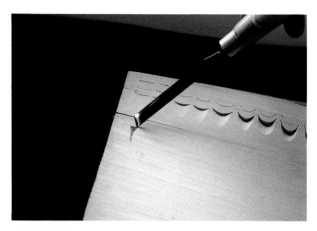

FIG 1.10 *No. 2 (Swiss No. 1S) skew chisel being used to clean out a corner into which a No. 1 could not reach.*

SPECIAL USES FOR PARTICULAR TOOLS

Most tools can be used for a variety of jobs but are particularly efficient in a few contexts. By continuously adding to your collection as needs arise or are foreseen or as opportunity offers, you can carve more fluently and crisply.

The No. 1 straight-edge is not much used in carving, as it is unsuited to making a flat surface which is wider than the chisel. It is generally used for stabbing a straight line (Fig 1.9). If the line is longer than the blade is wide, be careful to maintain the straightness by keeping a good length of the edge in the original cut before pressing down for successive cuts. This technique can be used in cutting letters, particularly for stabbing the centre lines of incised letters (*see* Chapter 15). Another use for a broad straight-edge is in finishing a large convex surface (such as the outside of a large sphere), since the corners are not as likely to dig in as those of a nearly flat gouge. One wider than 25mm (1in) is useful in these cases.

The No. 2 (Sheffield) skew chisel is useful for clearing wood out of corners (Fig 1.10), even for creating the inverted pyramidal pockets between grapes or berries in a bunch. However, it is also very useful for chasing a line or an edge, as it naturally slices through the wood with a knife action (Fig 1.11). A 12mm (½in) skew with a tip angle of about 70° is excellent for chasing letters once the centre lines have been stabbed in.

The No. 3 (Sheffield) (Swiss No. 2) extra-flat gouge is most useful in creating a flat surface; it works rather as a smoothing plane, which has its corners ground away so that they do not catch in the fibres. It is also used flute-down to create a gently convex surface.

FIG 1.11 *Skew chisel chasing the side of a groove, as in letter cutting.*

The Nos. 4–7 are gouges whose shapes make them generally useful, and they can be chosen for carving forms which they closely fit. A No. 5 or 6 is good for egg-and-dart mouldings (*see* Chapter 4).

The No. 8, being just less than a semicircle, is the most efficient at scribing circles and for cutting peas and the protruding eyeballs of fish and some birds.

The Nos. 9 and 10 are **fluters** – used for cutting fluting – but are also excellent for removing large quantities of wood. The No. 9 can be rotated in a cut without putting undue pressure on the edge. With a No. 10 this is risky, since if the tool has been driven in too far it is difficult to extract it without leaving part of the metal edge in the wood.

The narrow No. 11 or **veiner** is useful for cutting veins in leaves and narrow grooves such as those in hair. You should be careful when using one to cut wrinkles on a face or grooves between fingers, however, when it should not be used alone but as a preparation for a flatter gouge to make the convex surfaces on each side of the groove.

Carving across the grain with a large U-shaped gouge is a good way of quickly removing wood. If the corners are kept out of the wood there is little risk of splitting too much away. If one corner is kept under the surface of the wood it can be used to split surplus away, but it is sensible to see how far the wood will tolerate this treatment before trying to carve deeply (*see* Chapter 5). Some woods do not split easily, and those with an interlocking or otherwise erratic grain can play nasty tricks on the carver.

A V tool can be used to draw around outlines and also to make a clean junction between the ground and the vertical surface when a relief is set down. It is also useful for carving masses of hair and narrow grooves. Although it might seem suitable for incised lettering it is seldom successful, as one side of the gouge will nearly always be fighting the grain.

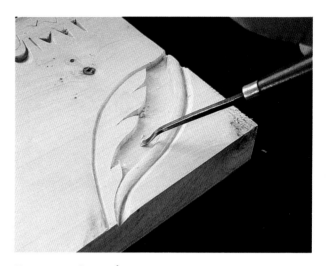

FIG 1.12 *Grounder.*

The bent tools are enormously useful when you need them. The English Nos. 21, 22 and 23 straight-edged short front-bent chisels are used mostly for cutting grounds in awkward places in relief carving (Fig 1.12), but I find the extra-flat (No. 24) and the 25 and 26 more useful than the 21. These flat and slightly swept bent chisels are known as **grounders.** One needs a variety of widths, including the narrowest possible for intricate relief. Modern manufacturers seem content with 1mm ($^1/_{16}$in). The higher numbers are useful for bowls, especially those which are deep or have a quick turn on the inside. On deep, bulbous foliage of the decorated style and on the inside curves of bar tracery (Fig 1.13) they are also essential. Bent veiners and fluters and V tools are useful for cutting grooves in the deep parts of rococo frames and for the hollows of scallop shells (Fig 1.14).

Long-bent gouges have a lower cutting angle, but as they swing up out of the wood better than a straight gouge they are excellent for wide, shallow hollows, especially where one needs to apply considerable pressure. They are easier to control than spoonbits. Some long-bent gouges are rather weak at the neck and should be avoided if they flex when pushed (Fig 1.15).

FIG 1.13 *Large spoon bit used to shape a concave inside curve.*

FIG 1.14 *Bent V chisel used to clean out the join between side and ground on an inside curve.*

FIG 1.15 *Two long bent gouges. The nearer one is badly shaped and flexes at the neck, and is difficult to use.*

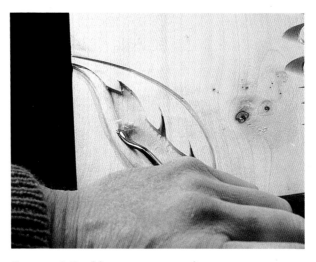

FIG 1.16 *Backbent gouge rounding a stem on an inside curve.*

The backbent gouge is much neglected but is ideal for making a convex surface, especially on an inside curve such as on a rope, tail or stalk (Fig 1.16). If too deep a one is used diagonal to the grain, there is a danger that it will tear the grain on one side. If you cannot bear to have an inside bevel on straight gouges, you definitely need some backbents, particularly of the flatter numbers.

MODIFYING CHISELS FOR DIFFERENT PURPOSES

Modifications may be made to the tools to suit particular needs. I and many other carvers find the Swiss spoonbit gouges rather too upswept (Fig 1.17), and, though it hurts to do it, it is sometimes wisest to grind a length from the end and resharpen so that it enters the wood at a

FIG 1.17 *Two grounders. Very narrow old English one in foreground. The Swiss one behind has too quick a turn to be useful except in very confined spaces.*

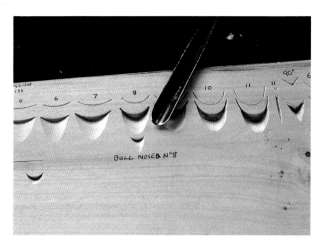

FIG 1.18 *A bull-nosed No. 8 gouge with its chip cuts. Note the deep marks left in the corners by the conventional No. 8 in the cut above.*

more controllable angle. If a chisel is to be pushed entirely by hand it makes sense to shorten the handle so that its head fits into the palm and the thumb can reach to press on the head while the fingers grip the blade close to the wood.

For letter-cutting it can be useful to have a 12mm (½in) No. 3 or 4 with a rounded (bull-nosed) edge for chasing out the inside surfaces of incised letters (*see* Chapter 15). A **bull-nosed** No. 8 leaves a finer mark with its corners when stabbed in (Fig 1.18).

A V tool does not cut well if it has a prong at the front, but nevertheless you can work further into a confined space with one. One which has a reverse rake, looking like two skew chisels fastened together at the obtuse angle, slices very efficiently through the wood but does not go far into a confined space (*see* Fig 1.6, bottom left). As so often, it is a case of swings and roundabouts. When you are experienced you may even invent tools of your own. Figure 1.19 identifies the shapes of the chisels and their cuts.

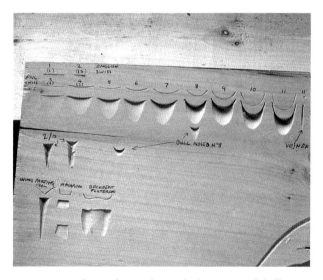

FIG 1.19 *The stab marks and chip cuts of different chisels identified.*

HOLDING THE WORK

In some cultures it is common to hold the carving in the lap or with the feet or with one hand. In the western tradition, however, the work is usually held on a work surface of some kind by a special device, leaving both hands free to control the chisels.

FIG 1.20 *A student standing at a carving bench with the elbow level with the top. The body is leaning to exert weight on the chisel. The carving is held on scrap wood by a paper join and the block is clamped on the bench.*

THE BENCH

Unless you are forced by ill-health or some other circumstance to sit down to carve, you should always stand. This means that you are more mobile and can put your weight more fully behind the chisel. The bench should therefore be of a height that allows you to stand without bending your back. For relief carving a good rule is to have the top of the bench at elbow level (Fig 1.20). For work in the round it is wise to choose a height appropriate for most of your work. If you have no bench it is possible to make a box or stand which can be clamped to a table. The workpiece can then be fastened to this by one of the devices mentioned below. The work surface should be stable and not move when the chisel is driven but, apart from being big enough to stay still, it does not need to be bigger than the largest carving you will do, with a little space left over where the few tools in immediate use may rest securely and be easily seen and picked up. Others may be laid out nearby.

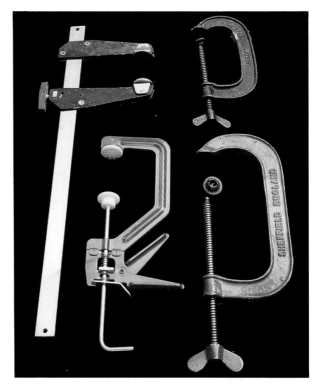

FIG 1.21 *Various clamps. From left: Jet clamp with long-reach heads and 670mm (26in) bar; Solo clamp; two G cramps, the bottom one having a loose button.*

HOLDING DEVICES

It is tempting to rush straight into carving without planning how the work is to be held. (Incidentally, it is worth mentioning here that you should always wear stout shoes when carving – sandals and thin shoes give no protection against falling lumps of wood and chisels.) Many means of securing work to the bench are now available (Fig 1.21). If you use a **cramp** (or **clamp**) there must be an overhang of at least 35mm (1½in) to allow for a grip to be obtained. Room must also be left below for the tightening mechanism to be turned. At least one corner of the bench should be accessible so that work can be clamped more firmly at opposite sides – work may swing if anchored by only one clamp.

A clamp should be strong and have its heads in line. It should have adequate reach and ideally should be able to be adjusted quickly. If it has a fine thread it will take longer to adjust and is more suitable for metalwork. When buying second-hand G clamps make sure that the buttons are not going to fall off.

The traditional woodcarver's vice or **chops** (Fig 1.22) is expensive unless you make it yourself. Kits are available. It can be held in a vice or clamped to a bench but is most effective when held on the bench by a special screw which allows the vice to be swivelled. You therefore need a hole in the bench top. The jaws are lined with cork and felt so that they grip well.

FIG 1.22 *Carver's chops holding work piece which has been squared at the bottom for a good grip. Note the bench screw that anchors it to the bench, shown here with wing nut undone.*

FIG 1.23 *Standard bench vice with quick release. Note the cheeks lined with thick felt or carpet tile to save space.*

FIG 1.24 *Bench vice with wooden dog in the moving head and thin metal bar holding a bench hook on the bench.*

FIG 1.25 *A bench screw.*

FIG 1.26 *A bench screw in use with a block of wood being used to raise the carving to a comfortable working height.*

FIG 1.27 *A webbing clamp holding an awkward piece on a saw horse.*

A conventional bench vice can be used (Fig 1.23), but it limits the angles at which work can be held. It is nevertheless always useful to have one, if only for preparing wood. Those with a quick release are more expensive but pay for themselves in convenience. If there is provision for a **dog** to be fitted to the moving head, and if dogs can be fitted on the bench, panels can be held without the need for clamps. This makes planing and carving easier as there are no obstructions above the work (Fig 1.24). Clamps and vices demand that the workpiece has at least two parallel sides. Unless the workpiece is inherently stable because it is heavy, irregularly shaped pieces of wood must have flat surfaces cut on them. If the piece can bear it a block can

be screwed on to the base, but the block and the workpiece must both be flat where they meet. At least two thick screws are needed if the workpiece is to be carved with force. The lengths of the screws and their positions must be noted to avoid the risk of carving into them or their leaving ugly holes on the finished article.

Another traditional way of holding wood which allows it to be easily worked all round is the **bench screw** (Fig 1.25). The pointed tip is screwed into the underside of the piece, then the body of the screw is pushed through a hole in the bench and fastened by a wing nut underneath. The work may be raised by adding a block between it and the bench (Fig 1.26).

Large pieces of wood may be so heavy as to need no restraint, though a saw horse may form a solid cradle which allows the work to be seen all round and rotated easily. **Webbing clamps** are excellent for gripping awkwardly shaped pieces (Fig 1.27).

Increasingly popular today is the ball-and-socket type of universal clamp, with the work screwed down to a faceplate that can be rotated through 360° horizontally and 180° in the vertical plane (Fig 1.28). The ball and socket joint is locked by mechanical or hydraulic pressure. A good one is

FIG 1.28 *A universal vice of the ball-and-socket type with a homemade face plate. The work is screwed on from underneath.*

FIG 1.29 *A bench holdfast in use.*

FIG 1.30 *A bedspring clamp holding part of a badly damaged outdoor sculpture while glue is setting.*

FIG 1.31 *A Jet clamp, showing the head fitting well on an angled surface.*

FIG 1.32 *A wooden cam clamp.*

expensive but very effective. It is possible to screw wooden bars with sash cramp heads on to the plate to hold panels, or even to screw on a carver's chops.

An old device which is still available is the **bench holdfast** (Fig 1.29). This enables work to be clamped from the middle of the bench. It usually comes with two collars which are let into the bench in different positions. The largest readily available in Britain will clamp wood up to 250mm (10in) thick, and has a reach of about 185mm (7¼in).

For relief work a frame can be nailed or clamped to the bench to prevent the work from sliding. The panel can be wedged while carved but moved around quickly. Alternatively, a frame can be made on a board which can be clamped to the bench, thus avoiding the need to make holes in the bench. In commercial workshops thin strips of mouldings are usually nailed to the bench. Another method is to glue a sheet of newspaper to a flat piece of scrap and glue the workpiece to the paper or use double-sided tape. This is particularly good with delicate pieces of relief. The carving can then be gently prised off with a broad, straight-edged chisel.

Holding is important whenever you need to glue wood, whether building up a block before carving or repairing a break. In the latter case the surface is often irregular or in danger of being bruised by the head of a clamp. An old trick of furniture restorers is to cut sections from an old bedspring and straighten them out to form rings. The cutting usually leaves the ends of the metal sharp, so that when the ring is opened out it will grip on an uneven surface (Fig 1.30). Be careful, however, as it will leave a mark unless the wood is protected. Another device which can grip on uneven surfaces or those that are not parallel is the Jet clamp, the heads of which can be loosened so the surfaces do not have to be parallel (Fig 1.31). Rubber pads on the heads reduce the risks of bruising and slipping. The **cam clamp** (Fig 1.32) has wooden jaws with cork padding. This is quickly adjusted and has a soft grip, useful on delicate objects. The single-handed clamp derived from the mastic gun is cheap and very effective, too. It does not exert as much pressure as a G clamp, but it is good for light work or in conjunction with another clamp.

MALLETS

A carver's mallet is round, the best being made of lignum vitae (*see* Fig 1.20) as there is a good weight in even a 50mm (2in) diameter one, and they last very well. Mallets are also made of beech, apple or other tough woods. A soft steel or a brass dummy used for delicate stone carving may also be used.

RASPS AND RIFFLERS

Rasps (Fig 1.33) and rifflers (Fig 1.34) are useful; those that are hand cut last longer and cut well. Surforms and dreadnoughts also help in shaping regular curves, especially on end grain. They are all,

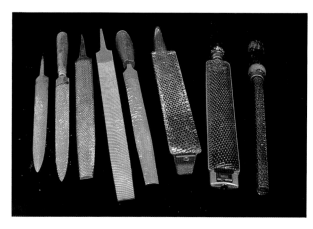

FIG 1.33 *Various rasps: from left, two hand-cut rasps, typically pointed; standard half-round coarse bastard rasp; flat and half-round dreadnoughts; three Surform rasps (flat, half-round and roundfile).*

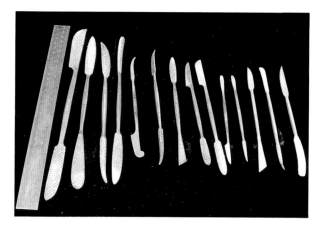

FIG 1.34 *Assorted rifflers shown against a 305mm (12in) ruler. All are handmade except the three on the right, which are coated with silicon carbide chips and will cut in any direction.*

however, best followed with a chisel finish as they can scratch the wood deeply. The alternative is the lengthy, boring and detail-blurring process of sandpapering down through several grades of paper.

MACHINES

There are now many machines available to speed the work: chain saws, bandsaws and rotary cutters attached to angle grinders for roughing out, and various small rotary discs, burrs and sanders attached directly to drills or on flexible drive shafts which can rough out and finish carvings, particularly in difficult corners. The effects they produce are different from those left by chisels, often less attractive. They are also expensive, noisy, dusty and less safe, but for large work they are very useful.

SHARPENING STONES

BENCH STONES

It is impossible to carve well without sharp tools, and you should buy sharpening equipment with

your first chisel. When starting out, unless you have access to a grinder and a buffing machine, sharpening has to be done the hard way, by hand. For this you will need a coarse, a medium and a finishing stone. Oil stones are most commonly used. The usual size of a **bench stone** is 203mm (8in) long by 50mm (2in) wide. Synthetic and slate stones are 25mm (1in) thick, but hard **Arkansas**, which is the best finishing stone, is very expensive and is now usually 12.5mm (½in) thick.

Washita stone, although it comes from the same quarries, looks porous and is much softer than Arkansas. Perhaps because Arkansas is a well-known name, the cheaper stone is also labelled Arkansas and the unwary purchaser buys the poorer kind. Genuine hard Arkansas is difficult to find. It is translucent, particularly when wet. Washita stone is not. Black Arkansas seems to cut slightly faster, producing a better edge, than the hard white Arkansas. It is not translucent. Hard Arkansas stones last more than a lifetime unless dropped.

You can also buy a **combination stone**, coarse on one side and medium on the other. The orange, India, stone is an excellent medium stone. The cheaper stones are too soft to last.

SLIP STONES

In addition to the bench stones you need at least one fine, preferably Arkansas, **slip stone**. Slips come in various shapes and sizes. The rule is to make sure that you have one which will fit inside your smallest gouge. It will do for your big ones, too, although you may prefer to have different thicknesses for wider tools. I grind an inside bevel on most of my straight gouges but even if you do not want this bevel you may at some time be forced to grind inside, and a Carborundum or India slip as well will save time.

CHEAPER ALTERNATIVES

There are various ways of saving money. A biggish Arkansas slip stone can be made to double as a bench stone if it is set into a block of wood. Slate bench and slip stones are cheap and are adequate for finishing, but cut the metal very slowly, while particles of grit or bits of discarded burr can get caught in the surface and scratch the chisel's edge.

Japanese water stones are excellent at removing the metal – indeed, the finishing stones quickly produce as good an edge as an Arkansas. They are comparatively cheap. However, they are not long lasting as they work on the principle that the surface is constantly worn away to expose fresh, sharp grit. Other disadvantages are that you need to dry the tools thoroughly, and any oil that finds

its way on to the stone clogs it. For finishing carving chisels a 6000 grit stone is quite sufficient and is far cheaper than the 8000 grit stone. The slip stones tend to wear into bumps and constantly need reshaping.

STROPS

Removing the burr after sharpening and keeping the edge keen are best done on a leather strop. A piece of dry hide will burnish the metal eventually but a dressing of chrome polish such as Solvol Autosol or Autoglym which can be bought from car or motorcycle accessory shops quickly removes the burr and polishes the metal to a mirror finish and the keenest edge. When the paste dries out it falls off the leather, so it is best to rub some tallow or petroleum jelly into the flesh side of the leather and then smear the abrasive paste in afterwards. A little will then last a long time. Pieces of leather glued around shaped strips of wood and dressed in the same way provide the safest way of stropping the flutes of gouges.

TECHNIQUES OF SHARPENING

AN INSIDE BEVEL OR NOT?

Not all carvers put an inside bevel on a gouge (*see* Fig 1.1), as it is a slight disadvantage when using an inverted gouge to make a ball shape. Its main

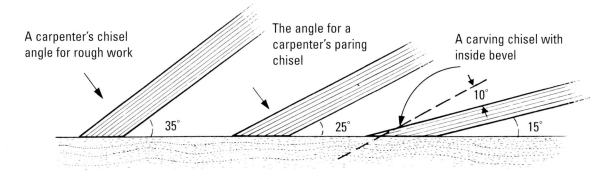

FIG 1.35 *Angles for sharpening chisels.*

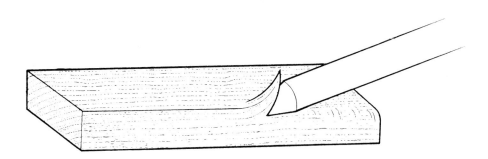

FIG 1.36 *It is possible to use the gouge flute-down if there is an inside bevel.*

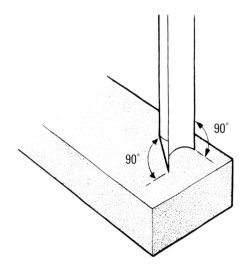

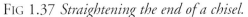

FIG 1.37 *Straightening the end of a chisel.*

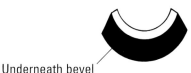

Underneath bevel

FIG 1.38 *Chisel edge after squaring.*

advantage is that it allows you to keep a moderately strong, sharp edge while lowering your angle of attack. This means that your thrust is not wasted downwards. Note that in Figure 1.35 the chisel edge of approximately 15° would be suitable only for soft timber. The inside bevel makes a combined angle of 25°. For hard use the bevels may be steepened. All angles are approximate. The inside bevel also means that an inverted tool can be used instead of a backbent to create a long, convex chamfer (Fig 1.36).

CORRECTING THE SHAPE

If the edge is not straight or is damaged it should be squared on the end of the coarse stone (Fig 1.37). If

you then look on to the edge you will see a white line probably varying in thickness (Fig 1.38).

PUTTING IN AN INSIDE BEVEL

If you intend putting in an inside bevel you will need to see bright metal right across. This bevel is ground in next. Put oil or water as appropriate on the slip or the tool to float off the waste metal. Rest the coarse slip stone in the flute with the end overhanging. Tilt the slip at a shallow angle (probably lower than 10°). Slide the slip back and forth, working from one corner of the gouge to the other, frequently checking that the back line of the bevel is parallel with the front edge, 1–2mm (^{1}/$_{32}$–^{1}/$_{16}$in) deep. It is easier to maintain

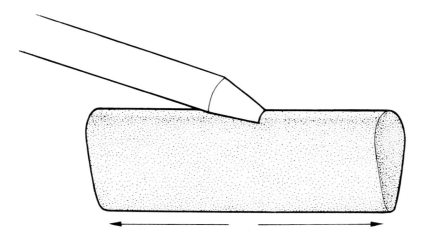

FIG 1.39 *Using a slip stone to create or polish an inside bevel.*

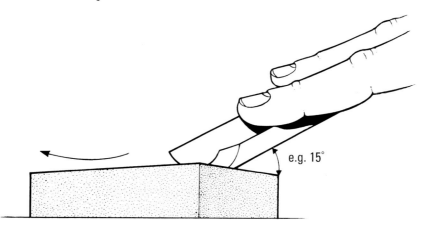

FIG 1.40 *The position of the gouge on the stone.*

the angle if you keep your elbows into your sides. If this is uncomfortable try resting the slip on the bench, invert the gouge and press it down on the slip at the designed angle. Then slide the chisel back and forth. Figure 1.39 shows the slip and chisel this way up. Both ways work.

GRINDING THE UNDERNEATH BEVEL

Next grind the underneath bevel on the coarse stone. To spread the wear on the stone always use the further side of the stone for your gouges (Fig 1.40). By the law of averages you should wear both sides equally, leaving the middle of the stone flat for plane irons and straight edges. Use the ends of the stone for squaring the edge (*see* Fig 1.37).

Do not use a figure of eight motion as it wears a hollow in the centre of the stone and quickly makes it impossible to use for accurate sharpening. Rock the gouge from corner to corner, travelling from one end of the stone to the other (Fig 1.41). This is difficult, as you must maintain a constant angle to the stone.

An efficient method of finding the angle at which to grind the underneath bevel is to hold it on the stone at the angle at which you want it to enter the wood. The most useful angle is when you grip the blade of the chisel with the little finger side of the hand about 35mm (1½in) back from the edge. Rest the edge and your knuckles on a flat surface. You then have a low cutting angle

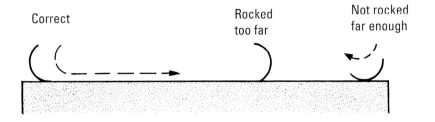

FIG 1.41 *Rocking a gouge from corner to corner.*

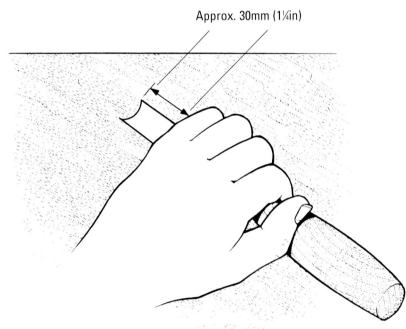

Approx. 30mm (1¼in)

Little finger and side of palm rest on the wood to form a pivot and an anchor

FIG 1.42 *Finding the angle at which to grind an underneath bevel.*

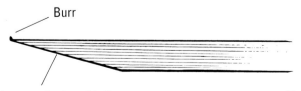

Burr

Make sure the bevel is flat

FIG 1.43 *The burr.*

(12°–20°) and maximum control (Fig 1.42). Frequently inspect the edge and the bevel to make sure that you are grinding evenly all over. The under bevel should reach the inside of the tool evenly. When the white line is no longer visible you will probably cause a slight **burr** on the top, as the metal is so thin that it folds over (Fig 1.43). Use the fine slip stone at the original angle to polish the inside bevel, thus chasing the burr to the underside.

If you have not ground an inside bevel you still need to use a fine slip to remove the inside burr. This you do by laying the slip flat in the flute of the chisel and rubbing it backwards and forwards without tilting it. On the medium bench stone polish away the scratch marks from the last stone. Follow exactly the same angle and motion. Periodically wipe the burr back to the underside with the fine slip. When the burr is very small and the coarse scratch marks are removed, finish on the fine bench stone, still working the burr back and forth between it and the slip until the burr has virtually vanished. Finally strop, always keeping the tool as you draw it along towards you at the same angle as on the stone, rocking it from corner to corner (Fig 1.44). With a specially shaped leather slip or a folded strop, polish the inside of the chisel by pushing the strop along the flute and across the edge. Strop alternately several times. The edge is tested lightly against the skin on a finger to see if it just cuts the surface, or by cutting across the grain of a soft piece of pine. Stropping about every ten minutes when working with the tools means you seldom use the stones.

V tools are especially difficult to sharpen. Treat them as two separate straight-edged chisels. There is no inside bevel. Do not buy a V tool of which the inside surfaces are not true. The groove at the bottom should be very narrow but nevertheless is bound to be slightly radiused. If you flatten the

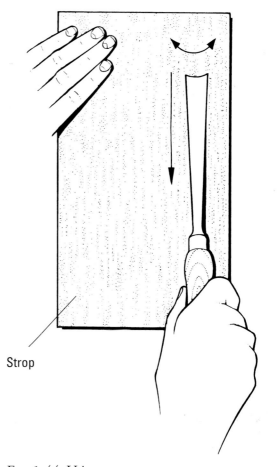

Strop

FIG 1.44 *Using a strop.*

end you will see a small white triangle on the edge at the bottom. This is removed by rocking the bottom of the tool until the outside shape meets the inside. Trying to make the bottom of the keel sharp creates a prong or beak, and carving with this is like cutting with a needle.

First attempts at sharpening usually leave the edge wavy or rounded (Fig 1.45). Keeping the end straight is less important than making the edge sharp right across.

GRINDING WHEELS

Because there is some 'give' in both strops and buffing wheels, eventually the angle at the chisel edge becomes inefficiently steep. It is not always necessary to regrind the inside bevel, but the angle of the under bevel must be reground. A grinding wheel can remove much of the boredom and frustration from sharpening. However, unless you have the skill and are prepared to retemper your chisels if you overheat them, avoid grinding on a dry wheel. If you use a vertical wheel take great care not to leave the edge hollow ground. It will make the chisel dig in. A straight or slightly rounded bevel is preferable. The best grinding wheels rotate horizontally and are water or oil cooled.

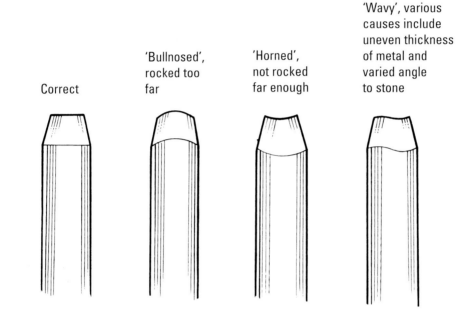

FIG 1.45 *Common errors when sharpening.*

CHAPTER 2

SELECTING AND BUYING SUITABLE WOOD

THE BEGINNER'S EXPERIENCE

There is nothing like a piece of deal (technically a particular size of plank of pine (*Pinus sylvestris*), spruce (*Abies alba*) or fir (*Picea abies*)) for teaching the direction of the grain and the importance of sharp tools. A wood like iroko (*Chlorophora excelsa*) or a knotty piece of yew (*Taxus baccata*) will develop strength in hand and arm and awareness of sudden changes in the grain. Lime (*Tilia vulgaris*) is too easy for the person who will carve whatever happens, but does give confidence to the less committed, who might be put off by a tricky or hard wood. Incidentally, deal, iroko and knotty yew are not recommended for serious carving.

THE WAY A TREE GROWS

Before considering the choice of wood it is worth looking at the way the material is made and its relevant, particular strengths and weaknesses. It is worth noting that no two pieces of wood, even from the same tree, let alone from the same species, will be identical, so any remarks about wood appearance and behaviour are inevitably general.

GRAIN AND SAP CIRCULATION

Because a tree grows upwards to the light and has to bear an enormous weight of branches, particularly when laden with fruit, snow or wet leaves, and has to endure both sudden and gradual wind stress, the main direction of the elements of which it is composed follows the line of the stem or branch. This is known as the grain. These elements, severally or together, have three main functions: to provide a means for sap movement up the tree, to provide storage of food in the form of starch, and to provide strength (Fig 2.1).

The sap returns down the tree in the layer between the wood and the bark, known as **phloem** or **bast.** Lime has great quantities of bast which used to be commercially valuable as a

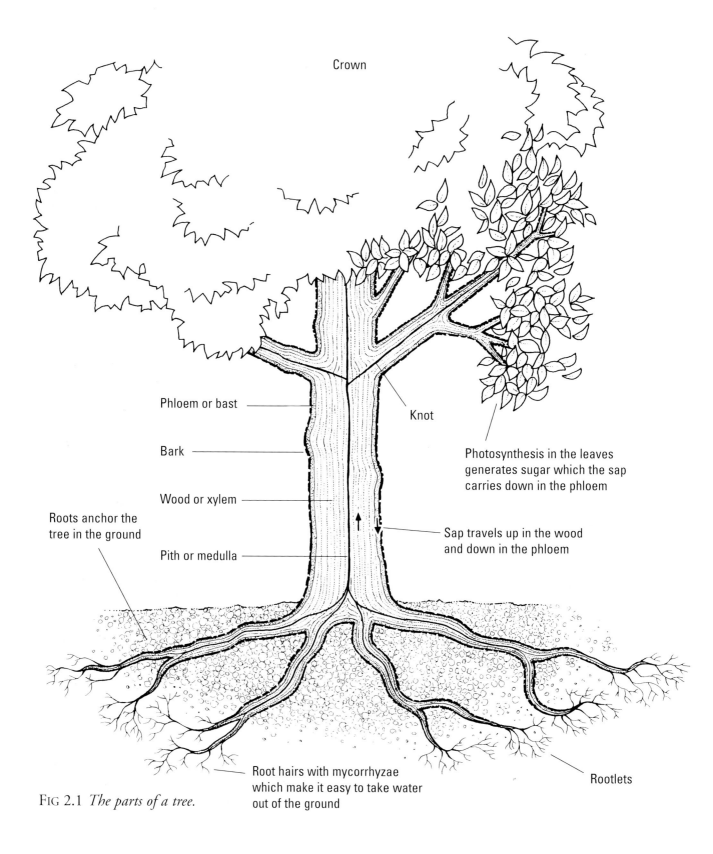

Crown

Phloem or bast

Bark

Wood or xylem

Roots anchor the
tree in the ground

Pith or medulla

Knot

Photosynthesis in the leaves
generates sugar which the sap
carries down in the phloem

Sap travels up in the wood
and down in the phloem

Root hairs with mycorrhyzae
which make it easy to take water
out of the ground

Rootlets

FIG 2.1 *The parts of a tree.*

FIG 2.2 *A piece of lime wood showing, from the front, the dark outer layer or bark, the pale-brown bast or phloem and the cream-coloured wood or xylem.*

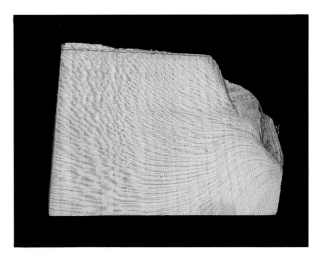

FIG 2.3 *Plane wood showing the rays. The figure on the left is typical and is why quarter-sawn plane is known as lacewood. The figure on the right is disturbed, probably by a knot nearby.*

weavable fibre, the bast often looking like part of the bark (Fig 2.2). The wood sends sap up the tree to carry minerals and water from the ground, and food from storage cells to make new growth, and to provide some of the ingredients for the creation of sugars in the leaf by photosynthesis. These sugars travel down, being deposited as food stores in the growing area of the stem. This is the **cambium** layer, which is the invisible layer of dividing cells between the phloem and the wood. The sugars are then used to create new wood, phloem or bark cells, and some are stored in special storage cells (**parenchyma**) which we know best as the **rays** (Fig 2.3).

THE GRAIN – ANNUAL RINGS

At the beginning of the growing season larger quantities of sap are sent up the tree. This means that the conducting cells tend to have thinner walls and larger cavities. Later in the year the cells have thicker walls as less sap is needed and strength is what is required. The result is that in the annual ring so formed there is a change of colour from the early to the late wood and, in some woods (conifers particularly) a marked difference in cutting. The **earlywood** of pine, for instance, is very soft and easily torn, whereas the **latewood** is dense and cuts crisply (Fig 2.4). Where there is a gentle transition, as in slower-grown softwoods and the so-called **diffuse-porous** hardwoods, this problem is not so marked. In tropical timbers the periods of growth are influenced by rainy seasons which may not even be annual. In many species growth is so even that rings are hard to detect.

EFFECTS OF GROWTH RING WIDTHS ON CARVING PROPERTIES

Ash (*Fraxinus excelsior*), oak (*Quercus robur* and *Q. petraea*), elm (*Ulmus spp.*) or any other **ring-porous** timber which has grown fast has a small proportion of the wood as thin-walled earlywood cells in relation to much denser, fibrous latewood, and is therefore much harder to carve than slow grown timber. Ash with 6 to 10 rings to 25mm (1in) is good for sports goods and tool handles, but is very difficult to carve when seasoned. Similarly, slow-grown softwoods are easier to

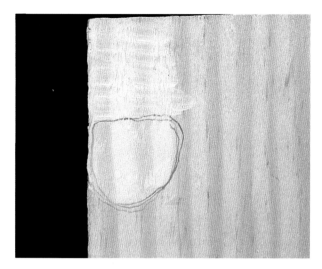

FIG 2.4 *A piece of southern yellow pine. The dark bands are dense latewood, the light are earlywood which tore easily when cut across the grain with a blunt chisel. The ringed area has been cut across the grain with a sharp chisel. The rest has been planed along the grain.*

FIG 2.5 *Slow-grown Quebec yellow pine (left) compared with the coarser texture of fast-grown southern yellow pine (right). The dark lines are resin ducts.*

work as the transitions from early- to late- to earlywood are less abrupt. Quebec yellow pine (*Pinus strobus*), for instance, a wood much used in pattern-making and frame-carving, is a delight, albeit an expensive one; southern yellow pine (*Pinus palustris* and other species), which has wide early- and latewood rings because it is grown in more favourable conditions, is very difficult to carve (Fig 2.5).

THE GRAIN – BRANCHES AND TWIGS

Very often the **pith**, or **medulla**, is visible in the centre of a stem or branch. Walnut (*Juglans regia*) is a good example (*see* Fig 2.21). Most branches and twigs begin from this. Some start only as an invisible line of cells waiting until the tree needs to make a new shoot in response to damage, while a few start from the cambium. The tree grows around the branch which also continues to increase in size (Figs 2.1, 2.6). The grain of the enclosed branch grows in a different direction, and

FIG 2.6 *A riven section of an oak tree. The pith is the dark fissure running down the right side. The grain around the knot is typically disturbed. This branch was cut off some years before the tree was felled and the wood has grown around it. The outside of the log shows no sign of the dead knot within. The arrow (lower left) indicates a ray.*

FIG 2.7 *The twisted bark on this ancient sweet chestnut will be matched by spiral grain within.*

there is considerable disturbance of the pattern where the two grains meet. This **knot** wood may look beautiful but can be very hard, and certainly means that the chisel entering the wood has to constantly change direction to cut cleanly.

THE GRAIN – THE FIGURE

The pattern of the grain, known as the **figure**, can be very attractive on simple shapes but can also be distracting in finely detailed carving. The figure of knots can be exciting, but other factors which affect the figure are the way the tree has grown. If you see the bark of the tree twisting you can be sure that the grain twists too (Fig 2.7). This is known as **spiral grain**. An even more awkward feature, more commonly found in tropical

hardwoods, is **interlocked grain**. This is caused by the wood spiralling in one direction for a year or two then spiralling in the opposite direction and so on alternately. This is called **stripy** or **ribbon figure** (Fig 2.8). In most timbers this makes clean cutting very difficult, as one side of the chisel may be cutting well while the other is tearing the grain. Cutting across the grain is the only safe method. For this reason you should be wary of the mahoganies (*Swietenia macrophylla*), iroko, afrormosia (*Pericopsis elata*), satinwood (*Chloroxylon swietenia*) (Fig 2.9), obeche (*Triplochiton swietenia*), utile (*Entandrophragma utile*), khaya (*Khaya ivorensis*), African walnut (*Lovoa trichilioides*) and many other exotic woods. I have met it in elm, oak and even in lime. It is

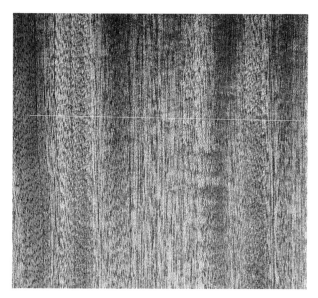

FIG 2.8 *Stripy figure in a mahogany-type wood showing light and dark stripes.*

FIG 2.9 *Satinwood when planed and sanded smooth has an attractive lustre in its cell walls. The different angles of the grain visible where it has been riven make carving along the grain virtually impossible.*

best to use this figure for simple, broad forms where a sanded finish could be acceptable.

Burrs are knobs growing on the tree, and are caused by insect, microbe or virus activity which stimulates the production of many leaf shoots or eddies in the grain. The result is that the grain grows in many different directions and is usually

FIG 2.10 *Ripples on sweet chestnut as they appear after planing.*

very beautiful. It is also unpredictable, and so has to be worked with the sharpest chisels or rasps and sandpapers or rotary cutters. Some burrs are rather like dense leather. The root of a particular French heather (*bruyère*) is carved into 'briar' pipes for smokers and is essentially a burr which is very pleasant to carve.

Another visually attractive feature which may pose difficulties for the carver is ripple figure. This is sometimes visible on the underside of a leaning tree and is commonest below a branch where it comes out of the tree. When the wood is cut cleanly it may look as though the surface undulates (Fig 2.10); the cells are holding the light differently as they rise and fall over what were folds in the growing wood. In a splintery wood such as yew this is hard to cope with, but a more cheesy wood can be worked easily and look good too.

DEFINITION OF SOFTWOODS AND HARDWOODS

The terms **softwoods** and **hardwoods** can cause confusion, particularly if one contrasts yew, which is a softwood, with balsa (*Ochroma pyramidale*), which is a hardwood. When the exiled court of Charles II was in Europe during the Commonwealth they

Softwood cells

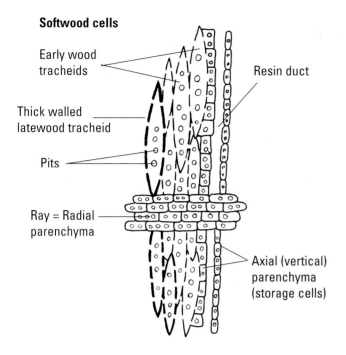

Early wood tracheids

Thick walled latewood tracheid

Pits

Ray = Radial parenchyma

Resin duct

Axial (vertical) parenchyma (storage cells)

Hardwood cells

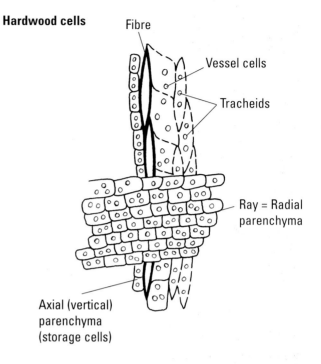

Fibre

Vessel cells

Tracheids

Ray = Radial parenchyma

Axial (vertical) parenchyma (storage cells)

FIG 2.11 *Typical softwood and hardwood cells.*

encountered beautiful, aromatic, light and easily worked woods in common use, and with the restoration of the monarchy in 1660 introduced pine, fir and spruce woods for construction and carving. The importers who brought these timbers in were selling woods that were soft by comparison with oak and the other commonly used native timbers. They became known as softwood importers and the name has stuck.

BOTANICAL CLASSIFICATION AND CELL STRUCTURE

It was only later that taxonomists classified the plants according to their ways of producing flowers and fruit. The needle- and scale-leaved trees were found to belong to one group, the **gymnosperms**, which means having, literally, naked seeds. The broad-leaved trees belong to the **angiosperms**, which have seeds in vessels. Softwoods are more primitive than hardwoods, having a less sophisticated cell structure composed mainly of

cigar-shaped cells called **tracheids** which conduct the sap in a zigzag fashion through connecting holes or **pits** in their walls and also provide strength. Softwoods contain very small **rays** and often have **resin canals** or **ducts** (Fig 2.11). Hardwoods, on the other hand, are principally made up of **vessels** which are short, hollow cells stacked one above the other to form a sort of pipe system, **fibres** which are dense, elongated cells and are more abundant in the latewood, and tracheids. Hardwood rays are usually visible to the naked eye and may be a millimetre or more thick and several centimetres high. The hardwoods may also contain gum, resin or latex **ducts**. Both types of tree have a certain amount of vertical storage cells (**axial parenchyma**). Yew and balsa, by these criteria, are respectively a hard softwood and a soft hardwood. Gingko (*Gingko biloba*) is an exception to the broad-leaved rule, having a fan-shaped leaf but being a primitive life form with the same physiology as softwoods.

Incidentally, a common mistake is to think that

softwoods are evergreen and hardwoods are deciduous. You only have to look at larch (*Larix decidua*) and holly (*Ilex aquifolium*) in winter to realize that this is wrong.

WATER IN WOOD

SAPWOOD AND HEARTWOOD: COLOUR AND CONTENTS

To use wood effectively it is essential to know the role of water in the life of the tree. A cross-section of a mature tree trunk usually shows a band of lighter-coloured wood next to the bark (Fig 2.12). This is the **sapwood**, and it is through this that the water moves from the ground to the leaves. As the tree grows in diameter not all the wood is needed for conducting sap, so the core or **heartwood** becomes inert. As this would leave it without means of combating disease or repairing itself the tree deposits waste products (the sorts of by-products of food that animals expel from their bodies as poisonous or useless) into the wood next to the sapwood to provide a natural preservative. Trees which produce the darkest heartwood are generally the most resistant to decay and woodworm. Timbers with light-coloured heartwood such as sycamore (*Acer pseudoplatanus*), lime, holly and birch (*Betula spp.*) rot very quickly if not cared for (Fig 2.13). Any sapwood, being light, also rots fast. Sapwood also contains starch and nitrogen which are readily consumed by moulds and other fungi, bacteria and woodworm.

POISONS IN WOOD

Because of the so-called **extractives** which give wood its colour and natural preservatives, many woods are regarded as poisonous, especially in dust form, occasionally causing an allergic response and, in some cases, cancer. The list is

FIG 2.12 *The cut end of a small yew tree. The dark area is heartwood; the light band is sapwood. The Y-shaped fissure is where the buttresses have begun to separate into three stems and is lined with bark. Had the tree continued growing for many years this fault would have been unpredictable from the outside of the tree.*

FIG 2.13 *A piece of spalted beech showing the zone lines where rival fungi have met. The wood is likely to crumble when carved.*

constantly growing. It is therefore wise to avoid breathing the dust of all woods.

THE CHEMICAL MAKE-UP OF WOOD

The main constituents of wood material are principally forms of **cellulose** and **lignin**. It is the cellulose element that gives wood its main strengths, while lignin confers stiffness.

WOOD AND WATER: SHRINKAGE AND SWELLING

Cellulose has the same chemical make-up as the glucose which is sent down from the leaves in the phloem, but is without one water molecule. Because of this, wood and water have a strong affinity, which means that wood finds it easy to adsorb and desorb water. If you squeeze a piece of freshly felled wood in a vice water will drip or even stream from it, but once the **free water** has gone, the wood still has **bound water** in the cell walls. This is called **fibre saturation point (FSP)**. It is when this water starts to be given up that the cell walls shrink and problems of splitting arise. The trouble with wood is that water is lost from the end and side grain at different rates and, in most woods, more rapidly from the surface than it moves from the core. The outside surfaces of the wood therefore shrink at a different rate from the inside. **Splits** or **shakes** (sometimes called **checks**) result on the ends and sides. As end grain loses water ten to fifteen times faster than side grain, splitting is worse at the ends. Even when the ends of wood are sealed with paint or wax this can happen (Fig 2.14). Typically, a length 125–150mm (5–6ins) is affected at each end. It is worth remembering that, conversely, dry wood can take up water and swell.

AIR AND KILN DRYING OF TIMBER

To reduce splitting most timber yards leave the logs for a few months to lose most of the free

FIG 2.14 *A piece of ash painted immediately after felling. Note the star shake around the pith and the other radial shakes that the sealing of the end could not prevent.*

moisture, and then convert them into boards of 100mm (4in) thickness or less. They are then **air** or **kiln dried**. Air drying involves stacking the boards in horizontal layers with piling sticks or **stickers** between them at approximately 600mm (24in) or greater intervals, each sticker being directly above the one below to avoid bending the boards. Hardwoods dry slowly, and are separated by 12.5mm (½in) stickers, while 25mm (1in) stickers are used for softwoods.

Air-dried timber is kept out of the rain and sun and is dry when it has attained throughout the moisture content that the humidity of the surrounding air will allow. Kiln drying involves an accelerated process in a chamber where the atmosphere around the wood is artificially controlled, starting with cool steam and moving at a pace set out in schedules varying with different timbers to warm dry air. This takes only weeks. The schedules are quite accurate nowadays but, because of the variability of wood, they are not infallible. Air drying, on the other hand, takes about one year for every 25mm (1in) of thickness, and is very unlikely to reduce the moisture in the wood to a state when it is dry enough to be safely taken into a centrally heated building. Some woods take even longer to dry, especially if kept in the log.

SEASONED WOOD – MOISTURE CONTENT

The process of drying the wood is called **seasoning**. Seasoned wood does not mean much unless one knows what it is seasoned for. If you buy expensively dried timber with a **moisture content (MC)** appropriate to a centrally heated house and use it for outdoor sculpture, you are wasting money. Conversely, if you buy unseasoned wood and put it into a dry workshop, you are inviting disaster. The MC of wood gives the weight of the water that is in the wood as a percentage of the weight of the wood material. A small sample is weighed, then dried in an oven for about 18 hours at a few degrees above the temperature of boiling water. When it has stopped losing weight the dry weight is subtracted from the wet weight, divided by the dry weight and multiplied by 100. The fibre saturation point, where all free water is lost and the bound water starts to be released, is around 30% MC. In a British summer, air-dried timber may go down to about 14%. A centrally heated house will require an MC of around 11%. This is useful information when one bears in mind that moulds and fungi require at least 20% MC to survive, and wood beetles cannot breed in wood at less than 10 or 11% MC.

SEASONING WOOD FOR CARVING

Many carvers acquire wood in log form rather than seasoned block, and wish to keep it in as large a piece as possible. The usual advice is to remove the bark, paint the ends and lay it horizontally on blocks where the outside air can circulate freely but the rain and sun cannot reach it. Keeping it in a shed or garage may ruin it if the place becomes an oven when the sun shines. Some timbers do not season well, but if they are first split or sawn lengthways into halves or quarters they will dry faster and with less splitting. They will probably distort, so if they are planed and glued into their original position when dried the pattern of the grain may not fit perfectly. This, however, is preferable to any other form of building up if the figure is important to the carving. I usually keep one or two pieces at least 450mm (18in) long in the log and cleave or, with the saw, halve or quarter the rest. If the ends have been exposed for a day or two I paint them with a disinfectant such as dilute Jeyes Fluid or a fungicide on the exposed surfaces to kill off fungus spores, which are omnipresent, before sealing the ends (Fig 2.15).

DRYING PROBLEMS WITH PARTICULAR WOODS

Some good carving woods such as laburnum (*Laburnum anagyroides*), holly, pear (*Pyrus communis*), cherry (*Prunus avium*), plum (*Prunus communis*) and apple (*Malus spp.*) are very dense and dry badly. I have found that, if these other conditions are observed and rot has not yet begun, leaving the bark on helps but makes the drying even longer. Apple and beech (*Fagus sylvatica*) particularly need watching for signs of woodworm. Another method is to rough carve the intended sculpture and leave it to dry or, if it is all to be very thin in section when finished, carve it immediately while green. This works very well with bowls. The beauty of this is that wet wood is much easier to carve. Sycamore and field maple (*Acer campestre*), holly, ash and beech are difficult to work when dry, as they are either hard or tough. I avoid beech if it is dry, for example, as the chisel almost bounces back out of it. This does not apply to the pinker, steamed variety.

OTHER PECULIARITIES OF WOOD AFFECTING SUITABILITY FOR CARVING

BUYING TIMBER – POINTS TO WATCH FOR

Timber merchants sell softwood boards sawn **square-edged (s/e)**. Hardwood boards are usually sold **unedged (u/e)** or **waney-edged**: that is, they still have the side of the tree showing, usually with the bark as well. If you ask for a piece 300mm (12in) in width and the board is wider in places, you may have to buy the excess, provided that that is nearest to what you want. Measurements are averaged by a rough and ready method, and serious defects are not charged for. Some yards will sell short lengths from planks but most do not like to be left with what are not popular lengths with the majority of their customers. Most will cross-cut them free to fit in your vehicle, but any machining is extra. **Planing all round (PAR)** usually adds 10% to the price. Most wood is required in thicknesses of 100mm (4in) or less, so it is not easy to find larger stock. When it is found it may not be fully seasoned. It is possible to kiln dry thicker stock but it is difficult and expensive. When buying timber it is worth asking for the moisture content, or at least finding out when it was felled and how it has been kept.

Wood with worm holes should be avoided as the worm may still be active, although the very small dark-lined tunnels of the pinhole borers

FIG 2.15 *The end section of an untreated piece of pine showing end shakes, including some ring shakes. The white spots are fungus mycelia.*

(Fig 2.16) are safe enough, and some tropical woods may have had an infestation of a forest longhorn beetle or termite that is not able to survive in the British climate. Blue or grey stains from moulds on the wood may disfigure it, possibly making it crumbly or **brash**. This state of **incipient decay** is also known as **dote**. Laburnum or walnut with light patches in a dark heartwood is probably partly decayed and should be avoided (*see* Fig 2.21). Rot may destroy the sapwood of yew, but as the white colour is often distracting from the pink, orange or red of the heartwood I am happy for it to have been eaten. Lime has a distinctive smell but may lose it if it is **dotey**. Slightly decayed

FIG 2.16 *Obeche with pinhole borer damage. Note the horizontal galleries and the dark staining caused by fungus planted by the adult beetles to provide food for their grubs.*

sycamore may feel no heavier than lime and in its sawn state looks like it. Merchants may accidentally sell it as lime. To test for dote and to see if the wood is too soft for carving, use a sharp knife or chisel on the end grain. If the sapwood is unsuitable the heartwood may be good.

THE STABILITY OF PLANKS SAWN IN DIFFERENT WAYS FROM THE LOG

Apart from shakes arising from drying, the carver in the round hardly notices if the wood distorts as moisture is lost. Carvers of panels, however, should be aware of how planks are cut from the tree. As it dries, wood shrinks tangentially or around the annual rings about twice as much as it does radially (Fig 2.17). It shrinks hardly at all along the grain. This means that the way in which it is cut from the tree affects its stability. A piece of truly quarter-sawn or radially sawn wood, that is where the rays run virtually parallel with the surface of a board (*see* Fig 2.3) and the annual rings strike the broad surfaces at about 90°, is the most stable form of wood. The surfaces should stay flat with slightly more shrinkage at the sapwood side than at the heart. This method of converting timber is wasteful of time and material, and various methods are used to reduce the waste.

The modern definition of quarter-sawn wood is that the annual rings meet the surfaces at between 90° and 45°. Boards with the annual rings meeting the surfaces at lower angles will **cup** because they shrink more on the side away from the heart. Quarter-sawn wood is more expensive. Most boards, however, are cut in sequence from one side of the log to the other. The only truly quarter-sawn plank in this case is the one including the pith. The others are **plain sawn**. It is important to remember that a plank, however sawn, left the same way up on the bench for a long time will lose more moisture from the top surface and will cup, making holding difficult. This is made worse if it has not reached equilibrium with the relative humidity of the air in the workshop before it was fastened to the bench. It is sensible when not working on a panel to turn it around or stack it against the bench so that it can dry on both sides.

FIG 2.17 *Cross-section of a cherry branch. The typical ways of converting the wood into planks were drawn on before the wood began to dry. The top half represents the way boards would be plain sawn. Note the cupping of the boards on the sides away from the heart. The bottom-left quarter shows why true radial sawing is wasteful. The bottom-right quarter and the next part of the bottom left show more economical ways of quarter sawing.*

It is a slow and risky business to return it to its original shape by wetting the dried surface – it may become so wet that mould spores take root and discolour the wood. The same damage can occur if wet wood is kept in a plastic bag to retard moisture loss. It is best to disinfect the wood first when doing either of these.

LESS OBVIOUS AND UNPREDICTABLE PROBLEMS WITH WOOD

Interlocked and spiral grain can usually be detected on the outside of a log or on a prepared piece of wood. Knots and inclusions of bark (*see* Fig 2.12) or even foreign objects such as stones, nails and arrowheads sometimes do not appear until the carving is well advanced. **Dead knots** sometimes rot while the tree is growing around and over the stump of a branch (*see* Fig 2.6), and you may unexpectedly discover them as cavities filled with crumbs and stains spreading outwards. It is to meet such eventualities that you should keep all offcuts so as to be able to patch the hole with matching grain. I have also encountered very hard, dark patches in some woods which quickly dent chisel edges. These may be **silica** deposits formed in response to damage to the growing tree (Fig 2.18).

REACTION WOOD

Timber merchants do not usually sell branch wood but they may sell wood from leaning trees, which can have the same characteristics. Yet another difference between softwoods and hardwoods is in the way they react to leaning (Fig 2.19). Softwoods put on much broader rings on the underside of a branch or leaning trunk. This **reaction wood** is strong in compression and consequently called **compression wood**. Conversely, hardwoods tend to develop more on the upper side. This wood is strong in tension and is called **tension wood**. Such wood is liable to distort and markedly change a carving when

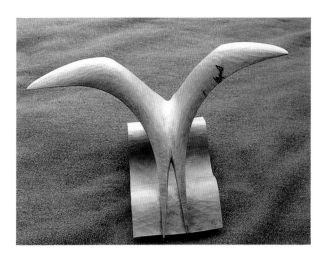

FIG 2.18 *Tern by Dick Onians carved in green field maple immediately after being blown down in order to eliminate splitting. The black mark is a silica deposit which is almost uncarvable.*

FIG 2.19 *Reaction wood. Compression wood of Cedar of Lebanon (left) and tension wood of ash (right). Note the off-centre pith and the irregular colouring. The right-hand side of the ash has been cut with a chisel to show the advantage over the dull sanded finish on the left.*

tensions are released by working it (Fig 2.20). Compression wood may be brittle and tension wood may be furry when rip-sawn. Reaction wood is usually recognizable because the pith is off to one side. Sometimes this is not so in hardwoods, but in these cases reaction wood often reveals itself by its unusual colouring.

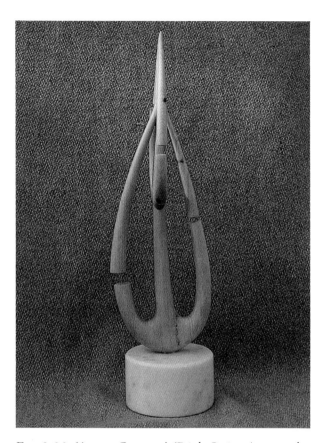

FIG 2.20 *'Arrow Crosstree' (Dick Onians), carved in compression wood of Cedar of Lebanon. The wood moved violently out of true within an hour of the gaps being cut.*

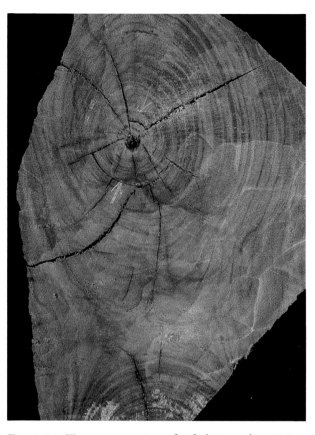

FIG 2.21 *Transverse section of a fork in walnut. Note the light-coloured diseased areas and the arrowed ring shakes. The many shakes around the typically large pith were almost certainly present in the growing tree.*

HEART PROBLEMS

The heart of the tree is often subject to problems and is sometimes removed by sawmills. Lime, for instance, may be rather crumbly in the **juvenile wood** around its heart.

Some woods such as lime, laburnum, oak, tulip tree (*Liriodendron tulipifera*) and walnut are also likely to have shakes radiating around the heart or, even worse, following the annual rings to form **ring shakes** for part or all of the ring (Fig 2.21). These probably arose when that part of the tree was still slender and subject to being whipped by the wind. Sometimes the tree secretes extra waste products in and around these shakes which can act like cement,

so that what appears as a shake is in fact no longer an open crack but behaves like sound wood (Fig 2.22).

SOFT WOOD

Very soft woods such as balsa and even obeche are almost impossibly difficult to carve except with the sharpest of edge tools, although they work adequately with rotary burrs and abrasives. Obeche also has an interlocked grain, which means that carving has to be done across the grain and will seldom be smooth.

HARD WOOD

Some woods, such as teak (*Tectona grandis*), contain minute particles of silica and quickly dull

FIG 2.22 *The brown lines on the near corner of this piece of lime are shakes which were repaired by the growing tree.*

FIG 2.23 *Padauk freshly cut across the end grain, but with varying degrees of brown where it has been exposed for different periods.*

the chisels but are pleasant to carve. Some are so hard, like African blackwood (*Dalbergia melanoxylon*), lignum vitae (*Guaiacum officinale*) and ebony (*Diospyros ebenum*), that they need very thick edges to your chisels, but have their reward in the colour or figure and their durability.

CHANGES TO COLOUR OF WOOD ON EXPOSURE TO LIGHT AND AIR

Woods like laburnum, mulberry (*Morus spp.*), padauk (*Pterocarpus spp.*) (Fig 2.23) and tulip tree dramatically change colour on exposure to light and oxygen. Ultraviolet light inhibitors only delay the change from bright colour to drabness. Purpleheart (*Peltogyne spp.*), on the other hand, is a pale pink on first being cut but quickly goes a rich purple. The usual rule is that light woods go dark and dark woods lighten on exposure to light.

THE RIGHT TIMBER FOR THE JOB

In choosing the right timber for a carving you have to consider colour, figure, ease of working, strength, durability, expense and availability in the required size. A carving with fine detail will not show as well in a dark as in a light wood, and a strong figure will camouflage detail. Dark and highly figured woods are best suited to simple forms with strong shadows in them. We all like a wood that is easy to work but sometimes this comes with loss of strength in the wood, or a too marked or a too bland figure. Sometimes, however, lack of availability may force you to use something difficult like yew, and you will find that the colour and muted figure amply repay the extra effort.

DURABILITY

Durability is a main consideration for outdoor work, particularly where water is likely to build up, as in ground contact. Light-coloured timbers may be safe for only a few months. English oak, yew and utile can survive up to 25 years, and teak and iroko may last even longer. The durability of most timbers is recorded in various reference books. Durability can be prolonged by thorough treatment with a preservative.

PRESERVATIVES

Modern preservatives can reduce the risk of rot but are expensive, except for creosote which has other disadvantages such as its dark colour,

FIG 2.24 *Vaulter carved in catalpa by Dick Onians. The strong markings of this ring-porous timber accentuate the movement. The strength of the grain runs along the potential weak areas of leg and arm. The short grain in the supporting arm is confined to a small area which is strengthened by the fixing pin that runs through it into the stone base.*

poisoning of plants and unpleasantness of application. However, the colour even of treated wood left exposed to the weather gradually changes to a silvery grey. Varnishes are of only short life, and as the wood moves moisture generally gets trapped under them and rot or mould staining occurs. Paint hides the figure of wood and can trap moisture in the same way. Danish and tung oils are best for keeping colour but need recoating every few years. Linseed oil, whether raw or boiled, tends to attract grime when used out of doors and will go black.

CHOOSING WOOD WITH APPROPRIATE STRENGTHS

When selecting timber for particular work the strengths have to be taken into account. Brittle or crumbly woods are undesirable where sharp edges or thin forms are needed. A tough wood like ash is appropriate where thin forms have **short grain** in them (*see* Chapter 13). It is best to arrange for slender forms to have **long grain**, that is, to have the grain running along them. It is not always possible to ensure this for all parts of a carving and risks may have to be taken (Fig 2.24), but the design can often be adjusted. It is sometimes necessary to add long, weak limbs, such as arms, not only for strength but also to make a sculpture larger than the available block. When this is done a wood with either no figure, like lime, or one with a wild figure, such as walnut, makes the join less obvious. The same is true when you laminate pieces to make a large block (Fig 2.25). Fudging joins with fillers can spoil a carving. Care has to be taken in the planning of any joints, as well as in the making of them, if they are not to be unsightly.

TESTING WOOD FOR ITS SUITABILITY

Almost all woods are carvable, and your choice will be affected by the time you are prepared to spend on a piece, the tools you have, the finished texture you want and the woods available. If you are in doubt the simplest test is to try a sharp knife or chisel on different aspects of the grain. Most woods work well along the grain. If wood is intrinsically soft or is diseased it will tear or crumble when cut across the side grain. Cutting across the end grain is the best test. You should beware if it plucks and crumbles. Rotary machines and sandpaper may be the only way to carve such wood. If you need great effort to cut across end grain you will have to be prepared to spend a long time on carving. One consolation is that if you want to sand it, it will take far less time than a soft wood. It will also last better.

FIG 2.25 *A carving consisting of four thicknesses of 100mm (4in) boards of jelutong, showing how the lamination is almost unnoticeable (Dick Onians).*

CHAPTER 3

FIRST CUTS: CHIP CARVING

THE GREAT VARIETY OF CARVING TOOLS

Although 'sculpture' originally meant carving there is now an acknowledged but unclear distinction between carving and sculpture. This difference becomes clearer when one compares the relatively few chisels used by many wood sculptors with the many shapes and sizes of chisel used by the traditional carver. Every chisel has been developed to perform certain tasks (*see* Chapter 1).

The carver competes against others with similar background and training, so time and efficient cutting are essential factors. The sculptor sells his unique vision and is less concerned with time. The carver fits the shapes of his chisels to the shapes he wishes to make. The sculptor uses the chisels to remove the wood he does not want. Imagine a line. At one end is the craftsman who is a wonderful copyist, giving only technique and nothing original: the model maker. At the other end is the artist who is all ideas and passion, but has no skill:

the conceptual artist. In the middle are the artist who is also a craftsman and the craftsman who puts something of himself into his carving.

The first project, therefore, needs to demonstrate how the shapes of chisels can be exploited. The following exercises are also instructive for those unfamiliar with the behaviour of wood.

Carving is done either by making one or more cuts steeply into the wood, followed by one or more cuts towards the first from the side, or by making short or long cuts along or across the grain. The first method takes its simplest form in chip carving. I shall deal with long cuts in later chapters.

REQUIREMENTS FOR FIRST CHIP-CARVING EXERCISES

WOOD

Use planed wood, not sanded, as grit may become ingrained in the surface and blunt your chisels. You will need boards for practice and a piece about 250 x 200 x 25mm (10 x 8 x 1in) for a decorative panel. Use straight-grained, even-textured wood such as oak, lime, mahogany, cherry, sycamore or beech.

CHISELS

You will need the following chisels (the widths are approximate).

◆ No. 8 gouge (possibly a No. 7), 3–12mm (⅛–½in) wide;

◆ No. 1 straight-edged chisel, 12–35mm (½–1½in) wide;

◆ No. 5 gouge (preferably a fishtail), 12–25mm (½–1in) wide.

Optional extras are as follows.

◆ No. 2 (English)/No. 1S (Swiss) skew or corner chisel, 14mm (½in);

◆ No. 3 or 4 (English)/No. 3F (Swiss) fishtail, 14mm (½in);

◆ a mallet, preferably of lignum vitae, 50–75mm (2–3in) in diameter. Figure 3.1 shows most of the chisels used for the patterns explained in this chapter.

Some brands of chisel are not altogether reliable. I recommend the Swiss Pfeil (Arrow) brand (*see* the list of brands in Chapter 1). They also come sharpened, although the extra little bevel on the underside is not ideal as they soon need resharpening. The bevel can be corrected then.

SHARPENING

You may not appreciate the trouble and expense involved in sharpening until you have experienced the contrast between blunt and sharp tools. You cannot carve well unless you can sharpen successfully (*see* Chapter 1). Even if your chisels are sharp you will need to use the strop regularly,

FIG 3.1 *Five of the chisels used for the patterns demonstrated in this chapter.*

possibly even before beginning. It is essential that the edge is sharp all the way across. The shape of the end is less important. Once you have learnt how to sharpen you will want to look after your chisel edges. This is done by preventing their touching metal or other hard materials, by not tapping them against the wood and by not driving them so far into the wood that it is difficult to withdraw them.

THE HEIGHT OF THE BENCH

Stand to your work for ease of movement and to put your weight behind the chisel. The correct bench height for small work is your elbow height. Fasten the work securely. If you use clamps, place them where they do not impede your work or pose a threat to chisel edges.

SAFE PRACTICE

Never carve towards any part of yourself. Both hands should be employed with the chisel. If the work piece is held in a vice it should be supported, because if it is loose and you carve hard down on one end the wood may fly up and hit you and the chisel may be deflected into you. Chisels are also dangerous to other people. Never wave them about, and when you are not using a chisel it should be placed gently on the bench.

THE FIRST CUT

The first exercise is to make what is the simplest of chip cuts. This cut is used to create effective detail on even sophisticated carvings, such as locks of hair on late medieval figures. A No. 8 gouge is used in this exercise, though a No. 7 will do almost as well.

The chisel enters the wood almost vertically, with the grain running from one corner to the other (Fig 3.2). It is leaned slightly to avoid undercutting and to leave the side of the cut tilted upwards to catch the light. The cut should go as deep as the depth of the flute (Fig 3.3). Note the position of the hands (Fig 3.2). Use a mallet if the wood is too hard. You will quickly learn how strongly to drive the chisel to reach the right depth.

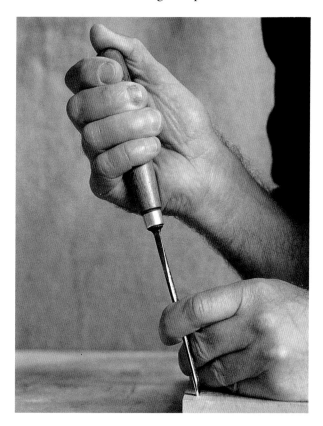

FIG 3.2 *The first, stabbing, cut showing the angle of the blade, with the flute facing slightly downwards, and the positions of the hands.*

The chisel is drawn back a little way and then slanted down to the bottom of the first cut. If the chip does not pop out at once, repeat exactly the same cuts until it does. Rotating the chisel at the end of the sideways cut helps. Next time, start the second cut further away at a shallower angle (Fig 3.4). In this photograph the chisel is carving along the grain. At the end of the cut the chisel's corners should be just level with the wood's surface. Practice is needed to find the correct angle. The classic mistake is to approach the stab cut from the opposite direction. If the chisel edge is square to its shaft the two cuts cannot meet at the bottom. If you need to create this effect you have to grind the end of the gouge to a bullnose (Fig 3.5). If the chisel's corners are submerged when carving across the grain the wood will split or fray. The same cuts should be practised along the grain. They can be varied to the 'thumbprint' pattern (Fig 3.6). In this case, the chisel enters the wood at a steep angle on the second cut. As it is pushed forward the handle is dropped quickly until the tool is travelling with the corners just proud of the surface. The neatest cuts will be produced if the No. 7 or 8 gouge has its end slightly rounded. This means that the corners of the chisel do not leave a heavy mark when it is stabbed down on the first cut. It does mean, however, that it is more difficult to cut easily to the end when finishing the 'thumbprint' unless one has an identical tool with the end left square.

A SIMPLE FLOWER

Hold the chisel as in Figure 3.2 and inscribe a circle by rotating the chisel on the surface of the wood, keeping the leading corner just above the surface and leaning the tool slightly across the centre. This is easier to do with a No. 8. If the chisel is pressed well in to start with, it stays easily in its own channel when it is rotated. When the circle is marked press the chisel in as for the first

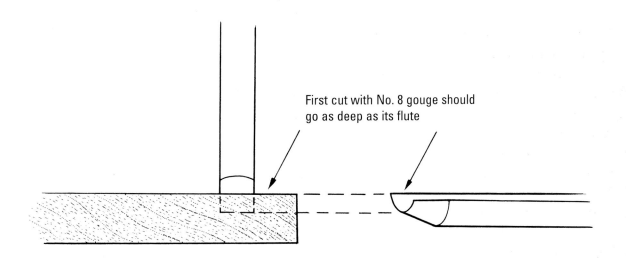

First cut with No. 8 gouge should
go as deep as its flute

FIG 3.3 *The depth of the stab cut.*

exercise. Cut in from the sides to form a flower pattern (Fig 3.7, top example). You will find that if you make the first tapering cuts along the grain the wood will crumble when you make the cuts at right angles to them. It is safer to cut across the grain first. If you use a No. 8 you will need to make small chip cuts in the angles before doing the next exercise (Fig 3.7, bottom).

To make the centre domed use the same gouge inverted. Cut along the grain (never across) from just beyond the centre, raising the handle as it travels until the edge rests on the original circle and the blade is vertical (*see* Fig 4.7). Repeat in the opposite direction. If the gouge cuts across the centre the height is reduced and there is a risk of leaving a sharp ridge. A round eye or berry and the pea or shot moulding in Chapter 4 are carved in the same way as this boss.

The chisel can create a saucer-shaped depression by entering the wood across the grain at a low angle and being swivelled around the centre (Fig 3.8).

If the circle is stabbed too deeply or is slanted under the centre the chisel acts as a wedge or a lever. These holes can be used decoratively (Fig 3.9).

TRIANGULAR POCKETS

The next exercise is to make triangular pockets. The straight-edged chisel is tilted down on one corner and leaned slightly away from the carver. A second cut is made at 90°, certainly at the same angle as or more than the angle at the end of the tool, with the corner lower where the two cuts meet. It is helpful to make this angle on a line and

FIG 3.4 *Cutting in from the side to meet a stab cut.*

FIG 3.5 *From the bottom: two correct chip cuts; the classic mistake where the chisel has been reversed; and how this cut can be made successfully with a special shape to the gouge edge.*

FIG 3.6 *Cutting a 'thumbprint' cut. After an initial steep entry the chisel travels along with its corners just proud of the wood to meet the stab cut. It is most important to keep the corners above the wood when cutting across the grain as here.*

FIG 3.7 *Tapered cuts made towards a stabbed circle to form flowers. Note the smaller cuts in the angles of the bottom example.*

FIG 3.8 *A saucer-shaped depression in the centre of the top flower. Note the domed boss of the bottom flower. The small cuts in the angles of the long tapered cuts are essential to let the inverted gouge go low enough to carve the dome.*

FIG 3.9 *A hole made by rotating the No. 8 gouge while pushing it well into the wood.*

FIG 3.10 *Triangular pockets. After the V is stabbed, the chisel is sloped down into the centre of the cut, starting with its corner entering the wood at one of the shallow corners and following that side of the V line until the edge meets the other line. The back line should occur naturally.*

to rest the chisel back on to a line drawn parallel. The chisel now enters at a low angle on the line on which it has just rested. One corner follows one of the stabbed cuts towards the low point, while the edge is aimed at the further cut. As the tool travels it should run along the back line to form a triangle (Fig 3.10). The behaviour of the grain may affect the direction of this cut. If the wood tears, the cut should be made from the opposite corner.

If the angle between the stab cuts is less than 90° a normal straight-edge cannot reach into the corner. A skew or a straight fishtail chisel is needed here.

If, instead of holding the chisel more or less upright when making the first pair of cuts, you cut straight in at a low angle to make this triangular pocket the wood will split and the corner look rough (Fig 3.11). To make all three sides slope you must first make three stab cuts to form a star with the lowest part of each cut in the centre. Each side is cut away as in the first triangle (Fig 3.12). As far as possible cut with the grain. It is difficult to take all three cuts to the same depth.

A similar form to the first triangle is made now with a No. 5 gouge. The final cut is made with the inverted tool to give a concave shape to the hypotenuse, too. To prevent the unengaged corner of the gouge from digging in (Fig 3.13) it is best to make a sharper angle with the first two cuts. It helps if the No. 5 is a fishtail. The serifs in lettering are cut using a similar technique.

A More Complex Flower

An effective pattern can now be made combining all these exercises. A flower is drawn up with compasses. The centre is cut as before. The petals are stabbed in with the No. 5 (Fig 3.14), but deeper gouges can be used with different effects.

FIG 3.12 *An inverted triangular pyramid. Note the three stab cuts radiating from the middle to the corners of the triangle.*

FIG 3.11 *Making the stab cut at too shallow an angle. The wood splits and the corner of the V will look rough. Here the chisel has wrongly bitten into the wood beyond the back line.*

FIG 3.13 *A triangular pocket with concave sides made with a No. 5 fishtail.*

The spaces between the petals are cleared as in the last exercise but with the chisel flute facing upwards, and as it is swung around with the corner following the line of the petal the edge should cut along the arc of the outside circle (Fig 3.15). As the wood is lime it is possible to cut against the grain here. The petals may then be hollowed and the boss rounded as before.

Although this is the logical order a better approach (which is more likely to preserve the edges of the petals) is to hollow the petals and round the boss before cutting the pockets. Another benefit is that one can then slope the sides

of the petals. This strengthens their edges and also gives an idea of the depth of the cut which vertical sides would not do. Interest is added by using the No. 8 gouge to make the petals dip in towards the boss (Fig 3.16). Note that the pencil mark in the middle of the boss is left. The very centre should not be touched when carving a boss. The mark may be gently shaved away.

The same pattern may be adapted to form stylized feathers, scales or tiles (Fig 3.17). In this picture a No. 8 gouge is being rotated to make the scales bigger. Deeper gouges may be used. Compare the difficulty a straight No. 5 gouge has

FIG 3.14 *Starting a more complex flower. The centre ring has been stabbed and a circle marked outside it less far away than the No. 5 will reach. Note the pencil marks around the inner circle. The diameters should continue beyond the outer circle. The edge of a petal is stabbed here.*

FIG 3.15 *The saucer-shaped depression for the flower to sit in is carved by making triangular pockets with the No. 5 gouge. To get a convex outer edge the gouge is used flute-up.*

FIG 3.16 *The boss has been domed and grooves are cut along the petals. The tool dips more steeply as it approaches the boss to give a good effect. Cutting the grooves like this across the grain can cause problems. The grooves could be made before the petals are stabbed in.*

FIG 3.17 *A scale being stabbed in with a No. 8 gouge, which is rotated to make a bigger scale. The bottom ones have been chipped out already.*

FIG 3.18 *A No. 3 fishtail being used to chip out the scale. A square-ended tool would have difficulty in reaching the corner.*

FIG 3.19 *Scales cut in oak showing the deep gouge used to stab the shape and the No. 4 fishtail used to hollow the scales. The scales on the right were made with the deep gouge cutting in from opposite sides to leave the ridge. The first cut is made across the centre; the second starts from the centre.*

in clearing the corners with the ease of using the No. 3 fishtail's acute angle (Fig 3.18). A skew chisel will go in even further. Different effects can be produced by experiment. In the pattern on the left of Figure 3.19 I have numbered the sequence of cuts and show the chisels used.

It is not easy for a beginner to get perfect results immediately. You will need to experiment with combinations of these patterns, and any cuts you have invented, to perfect your technique. Even if you are dissatisfied with your cuts you will have learnt some most important principles. It is also worth remembering that many repetitions of the same series of cuts impress the eye with their overall effect; imperfections of detail may escape notice. You could prove this by designing and carving a decorative panel (Fig 3.20).

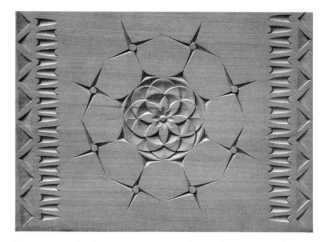

FIG 3.20 *A chip carving sampler. The cuts need to be practised and measured before a sampler is drawn out on paper. It can then be transferred to the wood.*

CHAPTER 4

CARVED MOULDINGS

The carving of architectural and frame mouldings, while resembling chip carving in the round, is a more sophisticated activity. Carved mouldings are found in or on old buildings and on furniture, which in the past was often treated as small-scale architecture, and on mirror and picture frames. Visit any gallery where old paintings are shown and you will find an amazing array of shapes carved into or applied to frames to help to separate them from their surroundings, to make them look precious and to draw the eye in. Even gilded composition mouldings, which you can often identify by the cracks at right angles to the direction of the grain, were pressed out of negative patterns carved in wood.

The commonest form of decoration is a repeated pattern cut into a moulded string with a curved cross-section. These mouldings were originally used by the Greeks and others not only to enrich their buildings but also to help reveal the shapes of strings of wood and stone often intended to be viewed in bright light from far below. For instance, the egg and dart moulding is carved into an ovolo or quadrant section because the shadows cut into the stone or wood make its profile clear, whichever way the light falls on it. Figure 4.1 shows this effect on various mouldings.

This chapter deals with the methods of carving five such patterns: pea or shot, egg and dart, ribbon and stick, strap or water leaf, and gadrooning.

Unless you can get the mouldings specially prepared in lime you will have to use softwood. Look at the ends to make sure that the annual rings are very close together. Ramin and other tropical woods are generally unsuitable, although jelutong can be used.

For the pea moulding you need a torus or astragal the same width as one of your smaller No. 8 gouges, or you can make your own as I describe below (Fig 4.2).

You will need a moulding prepared with an

FIG 4.1 *Various mouldings (from the top): an elaborate moulding on a cyma section carved in lime, originally gilded; a practice length of gadrooning in deal with U-shaped valleys between the gadroons (note the way the direction changes in the middle of the rail); egg and dart moulding with some of the gilding stripped away – the shadows around the eggs indicate the profile of the moulding (note the leaf at the right end used as half of the mask for a mitre joint); a practice piece of ribbon and stick in pine with an unsuccessful attempt at a leaf at the right end; a fragment of ribbon and stick with a typical leaf for disguising a mitre at the left end.*

ovolo or quadrant section for the egg and dart (Fig 4.3). It may have a fillet or strip of wood forming a narrow step on each side of the curved section.

For the ribbon and stick it is usual to use a dowel with about a quarter planed off one side so that it sits flat both on the bench and in its final position (Fig 4.4).

The strap or water leaf is a derivation of a leaf cut into a cyma moulding, that is, one with an ogee section. You may be able to obtain a straight cyma piece with or without fillets, but an architrave moulding can be adapted (Fig 4.5).

Gadrooning may be done on a shallow humped section, preferably higher at one side (Fig 4.6).

Many of these mouldings, especially those used on frames, will be gilded and so forms need to be cut more boldly; the gesso covers details rather like snow. One advantage of gesso is that repairs can be covered up and small gaps filled with gesso putty. The novice who is not too obsessed with the tidiness of his work may work more confidently in this case, and eventually be surprised by the crispness and liveliness that

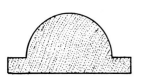

FIG 4.2 *A torus moulding in profile.*

FIG 4.3 *Ovolo (left, with fillets) and quadrant (right) mouldings in profile.*

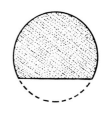

FIG 4.4 *A dowel in profile showing a portion planed from one side to enable it to be fixed.*

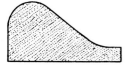

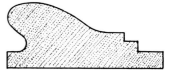

FIG 4.5 *Profiles of cyma mouldings (left and middle) with a section of architrave (right) which could be adapted to make a cyma.*

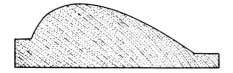

FIG 4.6 *Profiles suitable for gadrooning.*

comes out with practice. It pays to be brisk once you have worked out the order of cuts. You are unlikely to carve mouldings perfectly the first time; what matters here is learning the principles and learning to be decisive.

Holding small mouldings while working on them is not always easy with a clamp. Professionals generally nail them to the bench. Another method is to glue them down to strips of paper which are glued to scrapwood strips. Double-sided tape may also work. The clamps may then hold the scrap wood without crushing the moulding or hindering movement. The moulding is ultimately freed by a broad straight-edged chisel driven along the paper line gently all the way round, the paper then being removed. This system is much used when carving delicate pieces. The advantages over working directly on the bench are that you can stab down confidently to the background without fear that any slight hollow which might be in the bench will leave the edge unsupported and therefore liable to splinter, and you will not damage the surface of the bench.

Critical factors in cutting mouldings are the sizes and sections of the wood selected and the sizes and sweeps of the chisels available.

The examples shown here are students' first attempts and therefore look experimental.

PEA OR SHOT MOULDING

To carve a pea moulding you can use a prepared moulding. However, a useful bridging exercise from chip carving is to use an inverted No. 8 gouge with some inside bevel, or an equivalent backbent, to carve a ridge along the grain for a few inches. This ensures that the detail of the moulding is as close as possible to the shape of the chisel. It helps if the width of the ridge is established first and the wood on each side is carved down to the right depth with a V tool or gouge before shaping the ridge. If the wood is not straight grained your gouge may wander from its course and splinter pieces from the side. Once you have your ridge, mark off the width of the gouge repeatedly along it. You will also need a straight-edge (No. 1) as wide as or slightly wider than the gouge (Fig 4.7).

The essence of good moulding carving is to build up a rhythm. It is also a way of developing speed and deftness. You should practise one or two units out of each moulding before beginning the run to make sure you know which tools to use and in which order. Once the tools have been selected, spread them on the bench in a fan with the blades towards you and put all others away.

With the straight-edge a cut is made across the grain at each gouge-width mark. If the wood is dense or brittle the effect of driving the wedge-shaped edge of the chisel in all the way will probably be to pop the pieces off. Practice is needed to learn how far you can go. Travel from one end of the run to the other. Then, with the inverted No. 8 gouge, carve one side of each pea in the same sequence (Fig 4.7). As with the boss in Chapter 3, engage the edge with the wood just past the centre to avoid making the pea pointed. The chisel is pushed forward and the handle raised so that the tool finishes in a vertical position with the edge resting in the cross stab cut. If the shaping of the pea is done without the first stab or cancelling cut there is a risk that the next pea will be split off. Having travelled in one direction turn the chisel round and go in the opposite direction. Professional carvers usually become ambidextrous as this makes for speed.

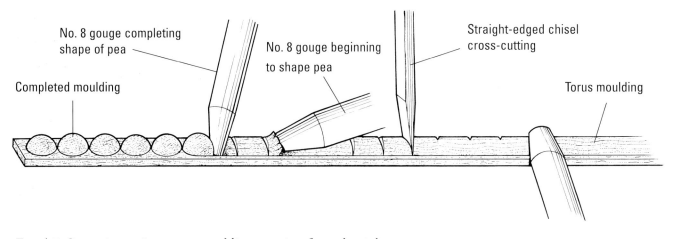

No. 8 gouge completing shape of pea

Completed moulding

No. 8 gouge beginning to shape pea

Straight-edged chisel cross-cutting

Torus moulding

FIG 4.7 *Stages in cutting a pea moulding, starting from the right.*

Any bits still left in the intersection should pop out if a skew, No. 2 (Swiss No. 1S), or flattish fishtail chisel is brought in from the side. Whiskers that persist will go if the gouge is held in the final position and pressed down with a rotating motion. It is always best to repeat the same cuts exactly or the work may appear ragged. The principles involved in this moulding are common to most others.

EGG AND DART

For egg and dart the following chisels are needed.

- No. 5 (or No. 6 English) about two-thirds of the arc of the moulded section – about 12mm (½in) wide for a 20mm (¾in) chord;
- a narrow gouge: e.g. No. 5, 6, or 7, 6mm (¼in) wide;
- No. 8, 2mm or 3mm (⅛in);
- No. 3, 4 or 5 fishtail, about 14mm (½in).

Before marking out the wood see what shape and size of egg you can cut most cleanly. Your chisel may leave you little choice. The Greeks favoured a long, flattish egg often sitting well inside its cup. The Romans made their eggs rounder and fatter.

The baroque style was similar. The tip of the egg in this case sits right on the edge of the cup. The width of the narrow egg is based on the radius of the quadrant. The width of the fat one is based on the chord. Experiment with the No. 5 or 6 gouge at one end of the strip. Hold it vertically with its side at right angles to the back line. Engage it lightly with the wood and slide it round in its own cut until it reaches the front edge, which will be the point of the egg. You may need to vary the angle against the back line to produce the best shape. Leave a reasonable distance for the cup. Decide how wide the band between the cup and the dart will be, then use the narrow No. 5, 6 or 7 gouge to mark the top of the dart about one-third of the way forward from the back.

Having marked off the centres of eggs and darts, mark in the outsides of the eggs and their cups. The first cut is a stopping cut with the chisel held vertically on the chosen outline of the egg at the back on one side (Fig 4.8). It is driven in with a mallet as far as is safe and this cut is repeated along the whole run. The same cut is repeated in the opposite direction, and then the top of the egg is shaped as with the pea, still using the No. 5 or 6 (Fig 4.9). If the side of the egg begins to move outwards, start to shape the cup. It is unlikely that

FIG 4.8 *The first cut on egg and dart. The gouge cuts vertically on to the outline from the back edge.*

FIG 4.9 *The egg is then rounded by using the gouge flute-down as for the pea moulding.*

FIG 4.10 *Cutting the cup. The gouge enters the wood vertically and the handle is dropped as the chisel goes down. This scooping cut gives a concave cup.*

FIG 4.11 *Marking the top of the dart. Note the chisel's angle of entry into the wood.*

the full depth will be reached the first time. Next, the chisel is held in the first vertical position and swung round to the point of the egg, taking care not to undercut it. When the eggs are beginning to appear rounded all over, the cup can be cut.

The gouge is put in vertically on the back outline of the cup and scooped down towards the side of the egg (Fig 4.10). The front part of the cup may be done in the same motion, with the gouge being swung round to meet the bottom of the egg. Practice will reveal how many times the process has to be repeated. The things to watch out for are that the egg should not appear spherical or be ridged and that the sides of the cup should be concave, neither too straight up and down nor sloping too flatly.

After the egg, the darts are shaped. These take several forms: little arrows, tipped-up tongues or the simplified points that I describe here.

First, the narrow gouge with a No. 5, 6, or 7 sweep is stabbed in to form a stop at the top of the dart about one-third of the way forward from the back of the moulding (Fig 4.11). The big No. 5 gouge is put into the corner of the cut, aimed radially (at about 45°) and slid around until it

meets the base line just to the side of the centre of the cup. If the chisel is driven horizontally at the end it will undercut the outside of the cup. Next make a chip cut to clear the waste (Fig 4.12). To shape the dart, invert the gouge and cut from across the centre, swinging it round to meet the outside edge of the cup. When cutting in the opposite direction, start from the centre line. This will leave a sharp rib below the surface of the cup rim. To make the point more or less sharp the straight gouge (or preferably the fishtail) is stabbed down from the side of the cup to the point of the dart with the blade turned inside or out (Fig 4.13). The No. 3 or 5 fishtail reaches further into the undercuts at the sides. Finally, a very narrow No. 8 gouge is used to stab out a small hole like a punch or drill hole between the stab cut at the top of the dart and the back line of the moulding.

RIBBON AND STICK

Ribbon and stick or pin and ribbon is carved with the sizes of chisel appropriate to its diameter. For instance, for a dowel about 12.5mm (½in) in diameter you could use the following chisels.

FIG 4.12 *After the rim of the cup has been stabbed in, a chip cut facilitates the shaping of the dart.*

FIG 4.13 *Stabbing the end of the dart using a No. 3 fishtail. The corner of the fishtail reaches under the undercut outside rim of the cup. Note the completed dart on the left showing a chip cut at the top.*

◆ Straight-edge (No. 1), about 12mm (½in) or 14mm (⁹⁄₁₆in) wide;

◆ No. 3 fishtail, 14mm (⁹⁄₁₆in) or the No. 5 used above;

◆ No. 7 about one and a half times the width of the dowel.

If you have a second straight-edge with a rounded end of the same width it will help when cutting the sides of the stick. It will also help if the No. 7 has a rounded end.

The ribbon twists across the dowel at about 45°. The intervals between the sides of the ribbon vary from design to design. It is sensible to let the size of the straight-edge with which the side of the stick is stabbed down decide. The ribbon may be any width, but is unlikely to be much wider than the exposed length of the stick.

After marking out, the straight-edge is used to stab vertically on the line of the ribbon across the line of the stick. About 2mm (¹⁄₁₆in) would be a reasonable depth to stab down to on a 12.5mm (½in) dowel. Once these stab cuts are made on both sides of the ribbon all the way along, the straight-edge that determined the interval is used to cut

FIG 4.14 *The first stage in cutting ribbon and stick, showing the straight edge used. Note that it is narrower than the interval it has flattened.*

horizontally to establish the top of the stick (Fig 4.14). The No. 7 is used on the edge of the ribbon that descends to the ground. With the flute facing the ribbon, one corner is placed a little way along the already exposed edge of the ribbon and the chisel is swung down to the ground while being pushed in (Fig 4.15). The side of the stick is then

FIG 4.15 *Cutting the side of the twist of the ribbon down to the ground with a No. 7 gouge. This acts as a stop cut.*

FIG 4.16 *The edge of the ribbon at the near side of the interval has been stabbed in down to the ground. The side of the stick has been stabbed down. Now the No. 7 gouge picks up the line on top of the ribbon at the far side of the interval and is stabbed in towards the side of the stick. The chisel should slope downwards when making this cut. It is slid around to stop against the back of the next twist of the ribbon.*

stabbed in with the straight-edge. Next, the gouge is started in at a flatter angle from the exposed edge of ribbon at the other side of the interval, so that the lowest part of its cut is in the middle of the interval and its edge ascends to meet the descending edge of the ribbon (Fig 4.16). If its end is rounded the tool easily meets the side of the stick, but if the end is square you will need to slide the corner of the chisel along the side of the stick to slice the fibres. If it has gone in far enough the straight-edge stabbed down against the side of the stick should pop out of the wood cleanly. The final stage is to cut the side of the ribbon where it goes up under the descending twist, stabbing down with the fishtail or cutting from the side with a skew chisel. Try to align the cut so that it matches the same cut on the opposite side of the ribbon. A very sharp, narrow fluter is needed to make the spiral grooves on the ribbon. (*See* Fig 4.1 for examples of completed ribbon and stick.)

WATER LEAF

The ogee section moulding or cyma requires the following chisels.

◆ No. 5, 12mm (½in) or more;
◆ No. 8 or 9, 4mm or 5mm (³⁄₁₆in);
◆ No. 8 or 7, 12mm (½in) or more;
◆ No. 2 (Swiss), 3, 4 or 5, 20mm (¾in).

These sizes will fit a moulding about 19mm (¾in) or 25mm (1in) wide. I describe here how rounded ends help some gouges to perform well.

The patterns again vary enormously (Fig 4.17), though most have a basically simple form which can be developed and enriched.

The cuts may be done in a variety of sequences. The edge of the leaf can be weakened by the shaping of its surface, so it may be safer to cut the dart first. The top of the dart is marked by a stab with the No. 8 or 9. If the gouge is rotated slightly

FIG 4.17 *Various examples of water leaf carved in lime wood, with and without gilding.*

the next cut is easier. The side of the leaf is then cut in with the No. 5. As the surface of the moulding is concave here it is helpful if the chisel has a rounded end, otherwise the chisel must be pressed into the wood and the corner slid around to the tip of the leaf. If you wish to make a rounder tip to the leaf a No. 7 may be used for all or part of the cut. In the example demonstrated here all the stab cuts were made before the surface was modelled (Fig 4.18). The dart is shaped in the same way as in the egg and dart. It is most important not to undercut the leaf edge with the first cut. When you cut the central rib by stabbing with the No. 2 or 3, and sliding it from the tip of the rib up and over the back, it is particularly vulnerable. It not only keeps the rib strong but also makes it read better if the cut slopes outwards (Fig 4.18). Again it helps if the end of the No. 2 or 3 is rounded to fit the

concave surface of the moulding. The top of the leaf is rounded into the rib with the inverted No. 7 and the lower part hollowed with either the same tool or the No. 5 (Fig 4.19). Here, too, it helps if the tool has a rounded end. It is risky but ideal to bring the rib right to the tip of the leaf. Figure 4.20 shows a completed run with some experimental veining on the right.

GADROONING

Gadrooning (probably from *godron*, French for a plait) consists of comma-shaped ridges usually with smaller ridges between them or U-shaped valleys. It is tricky as it involves sliding or pushing the chisels diagonally across the grain. Figure 4.21 shows the finished moulding with some of the chisels used. The requisite tools are as follows.

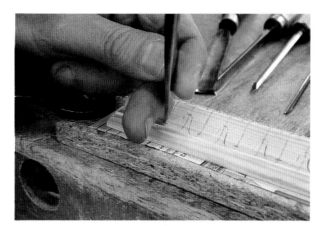

FIG 4.18 *The edges of the leaves have been stabbed in with gouges that fit. The side of the main rib is here shaped by an extra flat gouge which is sloped across the rib's centre to make its sides slope and be strong.*

FIG 4.19 *Cutting in from the side of the leaf to the edge of the rib with a No. 7 gouge, preferably with a bull nose.*

- ◆ No. 5, about the same width as the moulded section;
- ◆ No. 8 or 7, about 12mm (½in), to fit the nose of the gadroon;
- ◆ a narrow, deep gouge will help to set down between the noses of the gadroons;
- ◆ a skew chisel to clean out under the noses.

As with all of these mouldings it is best to experiment to see what your chisels will produce. The version with U-shaped valleys (*see* Fig 4.1) demands the utmost care and razor sharp tools if done in softwood, so first practise a simpler pattern. The example demonstrated was drawn with rather slender gadroons. As with other mouldings, the marking-out does not need to be detailed. A vertical stab along the side of the tail with the No. 5 which is then slid up and over to the ground at the front prevents splitting when the gadroons are formed. As it is the weakest element the small ridge should be made first, so stab cuts should be made on both sides of the tails. Do not worry if the tops of the small ridges crumble as in Figure 4.22. They will eventually be lower than the tops of the

gadroons. The sides of the ridges are then sloped, using the No. 5 first one way up then the other (Figs 4.23, 4.24, 4.25). The fronts of the gadroons may then be separated by notching with the deep gouge (Fig 4.26). The noses of the gadroons are rounded by using the No. 8 or 7 upside down. The tops of the gadroons are rounded by pushing an inverted No. 5, 6 or 7 gouge along them in the direction of the grain. A backbent is best on the inside curves. Care is needed to avoid cutting on both sides of the diagonal forms when doing this.

USING THE MOULDINGS

Having learnt how to carve them the next stage is to use mouldings applied to a frame or a piece of furniture. Special care has to be taken if you are not going to gild them. At corners the join is ungainly on most mouldings. To avoid this the mitre is disguised by a stylized leaf (*see* Fig 4.1), with the join forming a vein down the middle of the leaf. Simply leave a small distance uncarved at the side of the mitre, and draw on half a leaf which preferably echoes the

FIG 4.20 *A finished practice section of moulding. The sides of the rib are sloped outwards for strength. The leaf edges on the right have been scalloped in a typical pattern.*

movement of the carved moulding. Set down about 1.5mm (¹/₁₆in) around the leaf using gouges which fit the shapes, usually Nos. 3 and 5. The wood is then cut away around the leaf to that depth, interfering as little as possible with the carved moulding.

If the moulding is large enough the surface of the leaf may be modelled slightly by running a shallow gouge back from the tips of the lobes, curving towards the base of the leaf.

The resulting ridges enliven the carving. There are more elaborate treatments which can be sought out and copied. If the moulding is thick enough it will be possible to take a rebate. Otherwise, one or more mouldings may be glued to a sub-frame having a stronger joint than a mitre.

If you practise these mouldings you will produce not only useful pieces but also do wonders for your speed, control and confidence.

FIG 4.21 *The completed gadrooning with the chisels used.*

FIG 4.22 *Gadrooning drawn up and the small ridges stabbed in. It does not matter that the wood has split as it will be carved later.*

FIG 4.23 *A large No. 5 gouge shaping the side of the first rib.*

FIG 4.24 *The ribs have been roughed out and the large No. 5 is rounding the side of the first gadroon.*

FIG 4.25 *The ribs having been established, they can be cleaned up later; the shaping of the gadroons is damaging them. The No. 5 gouge was used flute-up for the inside curves of the tails.*

FIG 4.26 *Cutting between the noses of the broad ridges with a deep gouge.*

CHAPTER 5

FOLIAGE: COPYING A NATURAL LEAF IN WOOD

The use of foliage as a subject for carving goes back to earliest times. The religious significance of some leaves is clear, as with the vine and the trefoil in Christian art. The lotus too has a distinguished history, but the palm, the acanthus and many others have less obvious origins. At various periods, however, the leaf's function was purely decorative.

STUDYING LEAVES

Although it may seem easiest to make a simplified leaf to start with, it is always best to consult nature first. As an exercise take a number of oak leaves and sketch them carefully from various angles (Fig 5.1). Dried leaves are interesting from a carver's point of view as they curl up more and have interesting three-dimensional forms. Even though you may think that you 'cannot draw', drawing forces us to look and, most important, to see. Concentrate on the looking and seeing aspect and practise to improve your skill. It does not

matter if you make a mess. You are trying to learn and record the shapes, not make pretty pictures.

CHOICE OF APPROACH

The next stage is to consider how your leaf is to be carved in wood, whether as shallow or deep relief or in the round. You may, of course, start by incising the pattern on the surface with a V chisel, and as you model the surface gradually produce a leaf with full depth. This, however, is very time-consuming, and particularly so is the incised relief which reads from a distance as a work in the round. This demands enormous skill and understanding of the play of light and perspective. It is well worth aiming at but it is wisest to start with a literal representation.

CHOOSING THE WOOD

There is nothing to stop you making the leaf larger than life. The forms are less likely to be

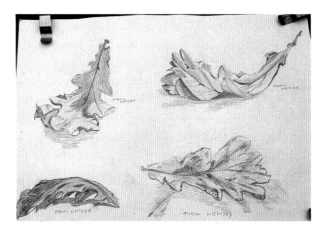

FIG 5.1 *Oak leaf studies by a student (Howard Spiers) before beginning the example carved for this chapter. He has tried to show them as three-dimensional objects.*

fussy if you do and should be more sculptural. The oak leaf which is the subject of this chapter is 216mm (8½in) long, 104mm (4in) wide, and 25mm (1in) deep. It seems appropriate, although not always easy, to make the leaf with the wood of the same species of tree. The main axis of the leaf is along the grain. This facilitates the carving and emphasizes the flow of the leaf. Quarter-sawn wood is the most stable but unnecessary for an exercise of this size.

HOLDING THE WORK

Having selected your wood it is essential that you plan how it is to be held and the stages of carving. The two obvious methods are to carve it as a relief, in which case the background may be held in a vice or with clamps, or in the round, where a rectangular plug is retained underneath or left around the stem or screwed, or glued with a paper join, to the bottom. In this case, once the accessible parts of the leaf are finished the block is unscrewed or the plug is carved down, gently shaping the underside of the leaf or the stem until so little remains that it can be pared off with a knife.

TRANSFERRING THE DRAWING TO THE WOOD

The safest method of putting the drawing on to the wood is to prepare it on paper. It is then far easier to change pencil lines, rather than trying to do it on the wood. The final drawing is transferred to the wood with carbon paper.

SETTING DOWN THE RELIEF

If the carving is to be a relief, after the design has been drawn on the surface the intended depth should be marked on the sides all the way round. Then the ground should be taken down to this level all around the outline of the leaf. If this is very notched it is best to cut out a simplified outline and set down the fine details later, particularly as some notches may end up near the ground.

Figures 5.2, 5.3 and 5.4 show three ways of setting down and roughing or **bosting** out.

The waste wood is carved with a deep gouge away from the outline and right to the edge (Fig 5.2). This may lead to more splitting off than was intended. It is also difficult to see how far down you

FIG 5.2 *The quickest method of setting down an outline, by carving downwards away from it. Note the ground line drawn on the side of the wood.*

FIG 5.3 *Cutting along the outline with a deep gouge or a V tool. The chisel cuts with the grain on the design side.*

FIG 5.4 *Stabbing down just outside the outline with a gouge which approximates to the shape. Be careful to prevent splits running from the corner of the chisel into the design.*

have gone in relation to the depth marked around the wood. It is, however, the quickest method.

A deep gouge, e.g. a No. 11, 14mm (½in), or a similar size of V tool, is chased around the outline carefully so that all cuts are made along the grain on the side nearest the design (Fig 5.3). Splitting caused by carving against the grain may lead to drastic losses or crumbled edges on the finished piece.

Gouges which approximately fit against the drawn outline are stabbed down with the mallet about 3mm (⅛in), away from the drawing, again making sure that no splits run from the corners of the tool into the leaf (Fig 5.4). It is most unwise to set down right against the outline from the start as you may undercut the design or tear the wood you wish to keep. The remaining waste wood protects the side of the leaf while the ground is carved down. Do not try to stab right to the ground in one go or the chisel may become trapped. Also remember that the chisel edge is a wedge and will crush fibres if squeezed in too far.

The ground is then carved from the side with a deep gouge which should be taken at right angles

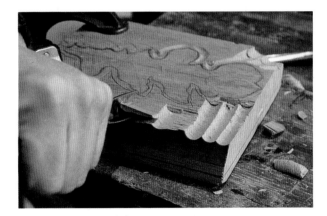

FIG 5.5 *A deep gouge being used to split wood away. Note how the gouge used like this removes three times as much wood for the same effort as one conventional cut. These cuts run into the aura of waste left around the design.*

to the grain. If the grain slopes it is thus unlikely to draw the chisel down below ground level. Indeed, by putting one corner of the chisel under the surface two or three cuts' worth may be split away with every cut, with little or no extra effort (Fig 5.5). If the grain is not parallel with the surface the cuts should be planned so the wood splits

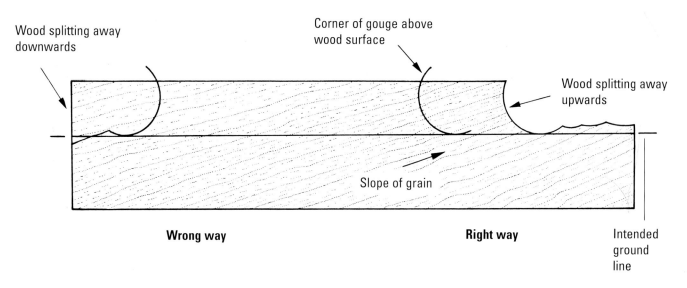

Wood splitting away downwards

Corner of gouge above wood surface

Wood splitting away upwards

Slope of grain

Wrong way

Right way

Intended ground line

FIG 5.6 *The gouge can remove plenty of wood in one stroke if the grain is arranged to cooperate.*

upwards (Fig 5.6). The deep gouge cuts down until the bottoms of the cuts are resting on or just above the ground line, giving a corrugated effect. Next a large No. 3 (English) or No. 2 (Swiss) is used to level the ground. You may need to use a No. 5 first. You still work across the grain but in the same operation you cut down close to the leaf's outline. You may have to make several carvings before learning the knack of making the vertical and the sideways cuts meet without leaving stab marks in the background. Various chisels will be needed to cut into narrow recesses (Fig 5.7).

Try to fit the gouges to the drawn shapes, but if your tools are a little too big it is sensible to modify your design to fit what your tools will do. The result will look as good and it will be far easier to achieve a cleanly cut carving. In the case of deeply notched leaves it is best to leave clearing out the ground in the recesses until later, unless the edges of the leaf around the notch are going to remain high. Similarly, a serrated edge is best left until last. Aim to make the leaf shape appear as if cut out with a fret saw and fixed down to the background before starting to model the leaf surface.

MODELLING THE LEAF

Unless you are one of the very lucky few who can carry a complete three-dimensional picture in their heads, it is safest to reach this stage first and then model the shape. It can take longer, but at least you know where you are at all times as the outline holds data about the surface of the leaf. Of course, frequent repetition of a design will develop a complete mental image: carvers in other parts of the world, for example, can carve, say, an elephant 76mm (3in) long in 25 minutes using hardish timber and rudimentary tools, because they have developed this visual memory. Possessors of this skill remove the ground simply to establish the depth to which the form may be modelled. Highs and lows and tilting planes are roughed out before the details of the outline are defined.

In the example illustrated here the oak leaf was set down in outline, except for the tighter indentations. The leaf is seen as twisted, with one side of the leaf lower near the stalk. In nature it is highly unlikely that the rim of the leaf would be parallel with the background all around, and unless you are making

FIG 5.7 *The ground is almost at its final level, cut evenly with a flat gouge, and a deep narrow gouge is setting down the notches.*

FIG 5.8 *The two gouges used for tilting the edges of the leaf and beginning to model the hollows. Note the sharp join between the ground and the vertical sides.*

FIG 5.9 *A V chisel being used to cut the central vein.*

FIG 5.10 *A gouge being used with the flute facing downwards to round the top of a ridge.*

the leaf into a bowl it is more lifelike if the rim is irregular. It also means a more three-dimensional use of the wood. The next process is therefore to rough out the highs, lows and tilting planes with a broad, flattish gouge (Fig 5.8).

MODELLING THE SURFACE DETAILS

Once the broad masses are established in the wood the line of the main rib is hollowed with a No. 11, 10 or 9 gouge or V tool (Fig 5.9). Here the tip of the leaf and the stalk are kept raised. This leaf is the

normal way up, so the veins appear on the top surface as grooves. Depending on the nature of the leaf, there may be ridges or grooves running back towards the centre from the major indentations in the leaf, known as **eyes** in conventional leaves. To make ridges, the deep gouge is driven along from the promontory or lobe of the leaf on each side of the eye towards the central rib, following the direction the vein takes in nature. If you cut diagonally one side of the gouge is going against the grain, but damage should be slight if you keep the corners of the gouge out of the wood and the edge is sharp. If it is difficult to push the chisel

FIG 5.11 *The top surface of the leaf finished, with the veins carved and the sides vertical to the ground. Note the shape of the leaf stalk.*

FIG 5.12 *Beginning the undercutting. Note the angle of the gouge and how it fits the curve of the edge of the leaf.*

straight through it helps to twist the tool so that the edge rotates, slicing the wood. This gives a much cleaner cut. The tops of the ridges are rounded using a gouge flute-down (Fig 5.10).

Once a ridge is roughed out it will need tidying. This will involve carving both from the edge of the leaf towards the centre and from the centre towards the edge in order to cut cleanly. This may mean using a bent gouge if the hollow of the leaf is deep. If you do not have one then a gouge sharpened with a steep underneath bevel and therefore needing no inside bevel may suffice. Alternatively, the edges of the leaf could be reduced to make the leaf less hollow. A narrow bent gouge was used to clear out the bottom of the veins in the example illustrated.

The carver here was making his first piece in relief and so was inclined to use smaller gouges than necessary. This can produce an interrupted surface rather like beaten metal. While this may be attractive or even appropriate, as in the case of a bumpy leaf, it is a good idea to practise making chisel cuts as large as possible – most carved objects are seen from a distance, and a heavily worked surface can look fussy or even be hard to read.

SHAPING THE GROOVES

It is tempting to shape the details of the veins by making simple grooves with a veiner or a V tool. One sometimes sees creases on a forehead carved in this way and they look somehow separate from the form they are on. This may be done in stylized work but when attempting to copy nature it is best to note that a groove is generally the bottom between the two ridges and therefore has convex sides which curve gradually down. A V tool was used here and the sides of the tool were used to create the rounded effect. A flattish backbent tool would also work very well. If the veins run right up to the leaf edges they tend to separate the leaf into compartments so it is best to fade them out at the tips.

UNDERCUTTING

Where the edge of the leaf rolls inwards, the outside must be shaped before the inside is undercut. Likewise, the rest of the leaf may not be safely undercut until the top surface is quite finished. This is an important principle in carving which only experienced carvers can afford to ignore. The carver of this oak leaf kept his options open so that when he realized that the edges of the leaf were still rather heavy he could make them more undulating and their turnovers more subtle. When this was satisfactory he undercut the rolled edges. To finish the top surface he carved the stalk and was surprised to find that an oak leaf stem is hollow on top, flaring slightly towards the end. This goes to show that, however much you may think you have observed something, there is still more to learn (Fig 5.11).

Before undercutting the outside it is essential to remember that what is being made is a carving of a leaf, not an actual leaf. To make it leaf-thin is merely to demonstrate patience, sharp tools and a steady hand; to make it look thin while keeping strength demands a sympathy with wood, consideration of future owners, judgement and skill. As this carving is most likely to be seen straight on it is only necessary to cut down at about 70° to the ground using chisels which fit the outline (Fig 5.12). Most of the work here was done with a large No. 3 (Swiss) or No. 5 which was used at the same time to clear the ground (Fig 5.13). Finally, the whole ground was cleaned by regular cuts with the large No. 3 cutting in the

direction producing the best finish. A large No. 2 (Swiss), No. 3 (English), would give a smoother surface (Fig 5.14).

SURFACE TEXTURE

If you see a perfectly formed and smooth carving in a medieval style it has most probably been done since the industrial revolution. Close examination of a real Gothic carving will show chisel cuts, irregularities in the modelled forms and uneven groundwork. Medieval work is more vigorous and the slight facets left by the chisels hold or reflect the light in a more lively way than a smooth regular carving.

The medieval carver had two advantages: he didn't know about things made by machine – the idea of identical items being repeated out of moulds or from jigs was unfamiliar – and he was excited because he was continually striving to perfect technique and learn new forms. The nineteenth- and twentieth-century carvers had very sophisticated techniques and, when making medieval forms, were not experimenting with anything new. They were merely demonstrating their technical superiority. Consequently,

FIG 5.13 *The ground cut in to meet the undercut using the same No. 3 gouge.*

FIG 5.14 *The final cuts are made along the ground, with the grain, to get the cleanest finish and to remove dirt.*

although the temptation to use a router to set down the ground is strong, there is no objection to its use provided you leave at least 3mm (⅛in) to be carved by hand. Likewise sandpaper, scrapers and rifflers should be avoided in this sort of work. Any scratches they leave in the wood make the surface dull, but even if these are all removed by careful papering so is the variation in the surface. What is left is a lifeless surface, which does not invite one to read the subtler forms, and pastryfied edges – rounded and heavy. It also takes much longer.

PROTECTING THE SURFACE

The surfaces of the wood now need protection against dirt, deterioration and moisture. Various finishes may be tested on the back or on an offcut which has been carved to show different aspects of the grain. Wax applied sparingly to all surfaces, including the back, will protect and enhance but should not be so shiny that all one sees is the light bouncing off the carving. Oil (raw linseed, teak, tung or Danish) may show up blemishes but will

give a richer colour and a gentle sheen. Two or more coats of Danish oil will make the surface too shiny and possibly rough to the touch. A sanding sealer used as a first coat can make the wood look like plastic. It may also raise the grain and make it bristly. This carving was finished with raw linseed oil and has a pleasant colour and sheen (Fig 5.15).

FIG 5.15 *The carving undercut and finished with linseed oil. The stab marks in the background would be removed by more careful finishing. The other chisel marks enliven the surfaces of leaf and ground.*

CHAPTER 6

CARVING TRADITIONAL FOLIAGE

The essence of art is to express what is intended as economically and clearly as possible. The essence of technique is to enable this to be performed. Sometimes, however, technique is wielded for its own sake and economy of form is sacrificed to a display of virtuosity. In this chapter I show how carved foliage may contain both economy of form and exuberant display. By copying from early examples the carver can learn from the discoveries of our ancestors about the design of ornament and many useful techniques.

A SUMMARY OF HISTORICAL BRITISH FOLIAGE STYLES

It is evident that although stonecarvings have survived better than wood, down the centuries styles were the same in both materials. A visit to Southwell Minster in Nottinghamshire will show that the thirteenth-century craftsman was master of both naturalistic and stylized leaves. The natural leaf forms, however, have been organized into bosses and spandrels to create artificial patterns. In the same series of carvings are contemporary 'stiff leaf' forms where the leaf is a very stylized trefoil of debatable origin. Its predecessor in Norman/Romanesque ornament was often a trefoil. In stiff leaf the very formalized ribs may unexpectedly dive into a groove in the leaf and disappear. When treated in wood the forms can be seen to be the product of various shapes of chisel (Fig 6.1). What it does have in common with nature is the flow, the tapering in of the lobes back to a central stem.

FOURTEENTH- AND FIFTEENTH-CENTURY GOTHIC STYLES

Through the Middle Ages various recognizable and abstract leaf forms were used, sometimes with the veins as the dominant feature: ribs for the underneath of leaves and grooves for the top. Sometimes the main feature was the leaf edge

FIG 6.1 *Stiff leaf panel copied in oak from stone original in Wells Cathedral, approx. 66cm (26in) high. Carved in oak by Michael Lewis.*

FIG 6.2 *Oak leaf copied from early fourteenth-century misericord supporter. Note the undulating surface and rib running along the switchback. Carved in oak by John Roberts.*

with the use of deep shadows in the eyes (the deep indentations) for 'punctuation'; sometimes it was the bulbous treatment of the surface undulating along its length like a whiplash or concentrically like ripples on a pond (Figs 6.2, 6.3). The Decorated style of the first half of the fourteenth century used very elaborate bulbous foliage moving in several directions at once. This ended more or less abruptly when the Black Death drastically reduced the population and weakened the economy to the extent that such rich work became generally impracticable. Thereafter ornament became simpler and styles changed to flatter leaves with more geometrical forms. Running bands of foliage on rood screens and the

FIG 6.3 *Plaster cast of poppy head (c.1380) from Lincoln Cathedral, showing oak leaves.*

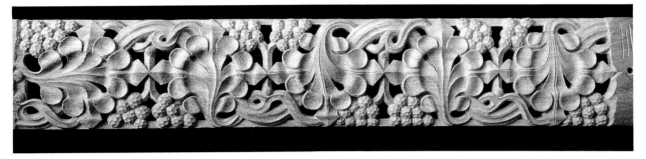

FIG 6.4 *Copy of fifteenth-century vine leaf running band. Carved in oak by Ashley Sands.*

leaf supporters on misericords as well as stone carving tell the story (Fig 6.4). Late fifteenth-century leaves sometimes give the illusion of bulbous foliage, although the leaves are in low relief by the simple expedient of having the ribs snake across the flattened leaf when viewed straight on instead of from the side (Fig 6.5). These ripples are sometimes heavily undercut to give an added idea of depth. The savings in thickness of timber and labour are obvious.

THE SIXTEENTH CENTURY

Hints of the Renaissance appeared in ornament in Britain early in the sixteenth century soon after the rediscovery of Greek and Roman ideas and art had changed the fashion in Italy. The acanthus and other new leaves and plants appeared. Forms became more delicate. The 'Roman scroll' became popular. In this, stems with leaves springing from them move from inside a central static flower or leaf motif into a spiral terminating at its centre with a fantastic flower which spills a tendril or weird fruit. Another motif on panels was a long, thin, usually vertical, stem with slender leaves growing symmetrically out from it and curlicues sprouting leafy grotesque heads, dolphins, birds or other objects. Unless executed by foreigners, however, British work lacked the delicacy of French and Italian.

PROTESTANTISM, PURITANISM AND THE RESTORATION OF THE MONARCHY

The Reformation and the Dissolution of the monasteries destroyed or dissipated into private ownership much ornament and art in the

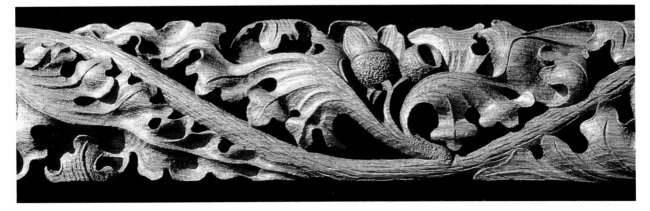

FIG 6.5 *Copy of late fifteenth-century oak leaf running band. Carved in oak by Mark Bridges.*

mid-sixteenth century and made many carvers redundant. The taste of the times changed, too, influenced from the Protestant Low Countries where the flat bands known as strap work and cartouches with scroll-like endings were popular. The Puritans from the last years of Elizabeth I's reign to the Restoration in 1660 discouraged ornament, and carvings became very simple. The Roman Catholic countries kept the

momentum going, but when the exiled court of Charles II returned in 1660 it brought not only a taste for the baroque style which had developed abroad but also an awareness of more tractable timbers such as pine, lime and walnut which thereafter became chosen above oak. Baroque foliage used many of the forms of the Renaissance but was more florid (Fig 6.6). The Roman scroll and the acanthus continued, but forms were heavier and leaves were inclined to begin from unleaflike scrolls. Because so much skill had been lost many of the carvings were done by foreigners. The carvings of Grinling Gibbons, himself half-Dutch, fall into the baroque style but also contain naturalistic or apparently naturalistic forms (Fig 6.7). The rococo style as seen in Chippendale frames and furniture took the scroll forms to an extreme. Asymmetry, arbitrary and irrational leaf forms, and slenderness are evident (Fig 6.8). The carvings by Luke Lightfoot at Claydon House in Buckinghamshire show this taken to extremes of quaintness.

FIG 6.6 *Baroque acanthus leaf originally carved in oak in 1685 for Tunbridge Wells parish church. Copied in Quebec yellow pine by Norman Barback. This ornament has the same movement as a Roman scroll without the flower in the centre of the spiral.*

FIG 6.7 *Part of frame carved in oak in Grinling Gibbons's style by Keith Ferdinand. Note the acanthus leaf used to make sense of the corner.*

FIG 6.8 *Rococo frame showing leaf edges to unnatural forms, scrolls and asymmetry, the whole having balance and rhythm. Carved in Quebec yellow pine by Deborah Hurst.*

CLASSICISM, THE GOTHIC REVIVAL AND VICTORIANISM

Contemporary with baroque and rococo were the classical and neo-classical styles as inspired by William Kent, 'Athenian' Stuart, Robert and James Adam and others (Fig 6.9). Some of these preferred symmetry and a more restrained use of ornament. Contemporary with the classical styles at the end of the eighteenth century, the Gothic Revival reintroduced leaf forms unused for centuries, but this time expressed in more manageable woods than oak or in plaster or composition. The nineteenth century was an age of recycling of old ideas but they were expressed by people emulating the regularity of things made by machines. Gothic, classical, Renaissance, baroque were all imitated with a stolidity and pedantic accuracy which, unless the carver was a natural artist, leave us gasping at technical ability but unstirred by anything more profound (Fig 6.10). Art Nouveau, which was an exciting movement at the end of the nineteenth century, used natural and highly stylized forms. The first half of the twentieth century added little to the interpretation of leaf forms in ornament, and although the last half has been averse to carved ornament except in reproductions and repairs there is a tendency for the public to expect literal representations (Fig 6.11).

CARVING CONVENTIONAL FOLIAGE

The comparative beginner at carving relief draws the detail on the wood and cuts down close against the outline and even preserves the drawing of surface details such as ridges and grooves as long as possible. We must remember, however, that the original carvers had probably made many of the same or similar forms before and, after setting down the general form, boldly carved the surface into high and low areas without stopping to establish the exact outline or surface detail. With many fourteenth- and fifteenth-century leaves the carver obviously set down a diamond, square or other geometric shape and then carved a series of grooves, often concentric. The lobes and any serrations to edges were then cut into these, probably without being drawn on first but carved directly. When you have carved a few leaves by painstakingly following drawings on the wood, you can improvise a leaf in the same style. The result will be much livelier and take less time, since for a practised carver the chisel is as

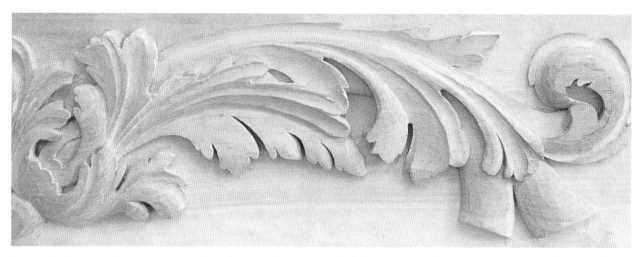

FIG 6.9 *Eighteenth-century acanthus from a Roman scroll. Note the typical turnover at the leaf end and the bifurcating stem. Carved in Quebec yellow pine by Keith Ferdinand.*

FIG 6.10 *Victorian carving (c.1860). Very cleanly and deeply carved, imitating medieval styles but lacking vigour. Also rather fussy. Brilliant technique.*

familiar a drawing tool as the pencil. The composition of a group does, of course, have to be at least sketched in.

I would urge you to find good examples of traditional foliage carving, study and draw them from different angles until you have clear pictures in your head. You are unlikely to notice every detail, so if you carve one of them it is useful to be able to consult it if you need to check anything. However, an obsession with absolute accuracy is unwise for the beginner, as you need to think for yourself and take some risks if you wish the carving to come alive. Copying slavishly is slow, deadening and likely to exaggerate any mistakes in the original.

KEY FEATURES

Things to look out for in conventional leaves are imaginary lines linking the eyes, and spiral or wavy patterns visible in the leaf edges or ribs or in the lobes of leaves whether seen from above or sideways. By chamfering leaf edges where the surface slopes up towards them you gain liveliness, a greater sense of depth and a stronger edge. Indentations between lobes usually have ridges running up to them. These ridges and other ribs converge but seldom meet, as this would break the leaf into islands and spoil the flow (Fig 6.12). Not every historical example that you see observes these practices but they are there in most leaves and have logic on their side. If, however, you find foliage with the edges all rounded downwards, bear in mind the saying of the late Arthur Ayres, who was one of the last great sculptor/carvers, that the English love an edge, the French cannot abide an edge and the Italians can take it or leave it.

FIG 6.11 *Rose carved in cherry for a memorial table, by Dick Onians.*

FIG 6.12 *Vigorous carving in old pine of Regency-style acanthus by John Roberts. Note the movement of the leaf ends, the turnovers and the strong 'punctuation' of the eyes, and the ridges converging but not meeting.*

CHAPTER 7

LINENFOLD

G othic furniture and panelling are out of
favour so there is little call for linenfold
panels in the commercial world. However, apart
from being attractive, linenfold is a most
worthwhile exercise for a relative beginner as it
teaches the use of several tools and is an
introduction to perspective in shallow relief. Even
experienced carvers find that it sharpens the mind
for problem-solving.

ORIGINS OF LINENFOLD

Why this motif, also known as parchment fold,
should have been so popular in the late Middle
Ages for panelling on chests and other furniture as
well as walls is not clear. Perhaps it was suggested
by the tapestry hangings with which draughts and
chills were kept out of the rooms of that period.
Some of the forms are extremely elaborate, with
many folds and considerable depth of carving
(Fig 7.1). Later forms were so stylized as to be no
longer recognizable as folded material (Fig 7.2).

FIG 7.1 *A student's linenfold sampler showing
luxuriance and depth of folds, largely the result of
clever perspective.*

FIG 7.2 *An example of late, debased, linenfold from a Welsh church. The colour was usual in the Middle Ages.*

MAKING ALLOWANCE FOR WOOD MOVEMENT

Linenfold was carved on panels which were then framed. The edges of the panels were rebated or tapered to fit easily in the grooves of the frame. The old woodworkers knew about wood movement and made allowance for expansion and contraction. If the panel is too loose it should be nailed only in the middle, at the top and bottom. It can then move sideways without risk of compression set or splitting. Compression set occurs when wood is restrained from swelling when dampened. The fibres are crushed beyond the point of no return. The classic case is of a mallet or hammer handle that is looser after it has been soaked in the head and then dried.

CHOICE OF WOOD

As linenfold is a form of optical illusion it does not have to be deeply carved, although there are examples which are 19mm (¾in) or more deep. It can be carved successfully in timber 12mm

(½in) thick. For the beginner's practice piece I suggest a board 25mm (1in) thick. It can, of course, be carved in any carvable wood, but as the original patterns were carved in oak it looks odd to us done in any other timber. Ideally you need a piece of quarter-sawn straight-grained wood at least 200mm (8in) wide by 250mm (10in) long. You may design your own pattern, but as a start I recommend copying old examples from actual furniture or panelling in churches or museums. If you are working from photographs then making a model in clay or plasticine helps.

PREPARATION OF THE RIDGES AND GROOVES

Although the actual carving of the linenfold pattern on the ends is what commands our attention and taxes our carving skill, the most time-consuming aspect of the work is the preparation of the section into which it is carved. The ridges and grooves of this are closely connected with the shapes at the ends. I have been told that the Victoria and Albert Museum possesses a horse harness with a linenfold profile cutter attached. This suggests that long ago someone had the idea of mass producing the panels. A long board would have been moulded by the cutter being drawn along like a plane. It would then have been cut into appropriate lengths. Indeed, if you are making several panels you can maintain consistency by running the moulding all along a board which is then cut to lengths to save time. Close examination of old examples will show, however, that mostly the section was cut by hand with chisels. Saw cuts along the lower grooves help to keep the chisels in a straight line. If you have the moulding planes known as 'hollows' and 'rounds' they can make the cuts to the ground level, not allowing for the lowest fold of the linen. If the panel is thick enough it may be possible to push the surrounding ground down to allow an extra depth, but if it is already prepared for fixing in its frame the mistake may be irremediable.

First, the depth of the carving must be marked around the sides of the board and a template cut for the end section. If this represents half the width and the centre of the board is carefully marked at each end it is possible to use the same template, reversing where necessary, to mark the pattern exactly on each end. Lines are then drawn on the surface of the board to join the ends of the board where there are sharp ridges or the cuts fall straight down, as at the sides and ends and along the deep folds. Saw cuts may also be made into the deepest parts of hollows to guide a moulding plane or gouge. Tenon saws and planes are liable to dip at the beginning and end of a run unless great care is taken. It is therefore wisest to cut down the sides of the ornament to ground level but leave the ends until the ridges and grooves have been shaped. In the examples shown here the sides and ends have been set down before the pattern has been marked on the ends. They were set down with a tenon saw, though a shoulder or rebate plane could be used. Figures 7.4, 7.5 and 7.6 show the furrows being cut with narrow straight-edged chisel, gouge and hollowing plane, the last with a fence clamped as a guide.

FIG 7.3 *Drawings of a linenfold pattern by a student before preparing the wood. Note the thickness of the material allowed for in the end elevation.*

more evenly but they can be hard to control even if a fence is clamped on, and they can tear the grain. If the medieval carvers had had routers they would probably have used them, but the effect would have appeared very regular and lifeless. It is best to do it by hand.

Whatever its later development, the feature which provided linenfold with its name is the continuous sheet with its material folded back on itself. It is therefore important to allow for the thickness of the material. The edge may not be as clearly defined as in Figure 7.3, but each step down has to be of a reasonable thickness. When these panels were being made in quantity this rule was not always observed. A common mistake, however, is to make saw cuts and channels down

TWO COMMON MISTAKES

It is quite unnecessary to meticulously draw the pattern on the surface, as the drawing will be removed by the first passes with the planes. It should be possible to carve the ends before running the furrows but it would be a thankless task.

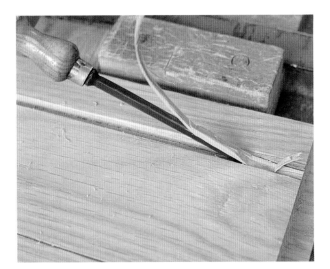

FIG 7.4 *The ground level has been sawn down at the sides and ends and a narrow, straight-edged chisel is carving a channel along saw cuts which are used as a guide. Note the sawcut in the foreground.*

Another mistake sometimes made is to assume that all lines drawn are cut against vertically. If saw cuts were made along the lines of the ridges that appear in Figure 7.5 the design would need to be drastically altered.

THE LOGIC OF PERSPECTIVE

If you take a sheet of card and curl it as in Figure 7.7 and then stand it on end you will observe how the parts that are nearest to you appear lower down. This is a rule that usually obtains with linenfold, although there are plenty of examples where the carver's sense of design has got the better of his sense of perspective (*see* Fig 7.3).

In the very stylized sixteenth-century and early seventeenth-century designs (*see* Fig 7.2), where the continuity of the material has been replaced by a simple series of vertical grooves and ridges, the top edge is carved into points and hollows but the bottom edge is often straight. The older designs have a carved bottom edge but the logic of

FIG 7.5 *A deep gouge carving a deep fold. The saw cuts do not always follow every line drawn along the surface.*

FIG 7.6 *A moulding plane used against a fence clamped on the wood to cut a hollow.*

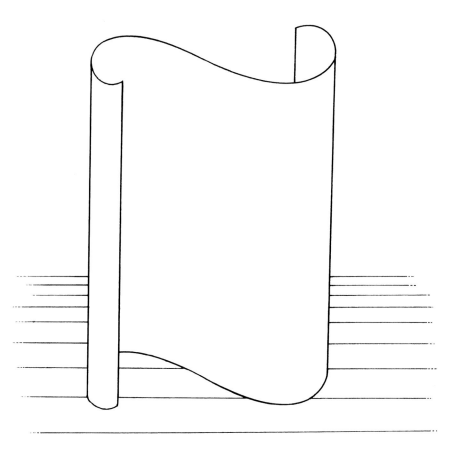

FIG 7.7 *This is how a piece of card would look if folded and stood on end. The elements nearer the viewer appear lower down the page.*

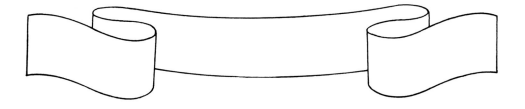

FIG 7.8 *The same perspective has to be maintained on both top and bottom edges of a narrow band.*

perspective is lost as the bottom edge is a mirror image of the top. If it is done logically it is difficult to carve and reads badly. Perhaps the mirror image was used so that the panel could easily be reversed. If you carve a scroll or ribbon the top and bottom edges are so close together that perspective has to be maintained (Fig 7.8).

MARKING THE END PATTERN: MORE OPPORTUNITIES FOR MISTAKES

Once the profile has been cut cleanly from end to end the pattern should be drawn on the ends (Fig 7.9). Another mistake sometimes perpetrated is accidentally to omit one of the lines marking the side edges of a lower fold of material (Fig 7.10). Notice in Figure 7.9 the arrow drawn to indicate the line of the lower

FIG 7.9 *The pattern of the end drawn on to one side of a panel. It is a waste of time to draw it on the left side which still needs to be planed.*

Omitted line

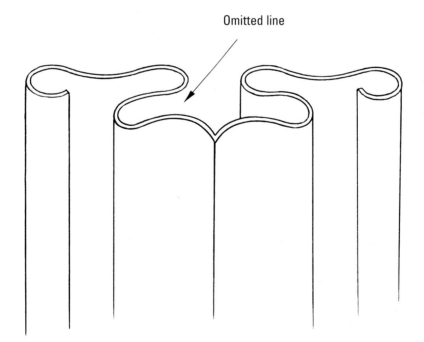

FIG 7.10 *The omission of the line here when the pattern is drawn on the wood is usually disastrous. After the outline of the end has been set down to the ground, modelling can begin.*

fold. If these are forgotten irreversible damage is caused when the shape of the end is set down to the ground. Yet another error is to fail to keep the lines parallel.

CARVING THE END PATTERN

Only when the ground has been set down tightly against the pattern can the modelling of the folds begin. The carving of the ends of the folds is simple once you have done it, but it is initially confusing. Begin by carving the top level first. If a vertical cut is made all the way along the line you get a stepped edge, whereas you want the edge to be continuous. It is therefore important to stab vertically until just before the curve of the fold begins to swing forwards (Fig 7.11). Use gouges that fit the shapes drawn on the wood. As the wood is oak it is unlikely that the cut will be too deep. If the actual edges of the folds have been drawn on the end grain you can see how deep to go. The next cut is the crucial one. With a No. 8, 9 or 10 gouge, cut across from the outside of the fold with the corner nearest the end of the panel

under the grain (Fig 7.12). If the grain is straight the waste will split away down to the top of the next fold. The edge of the material will be seen to slope continuously to the next level. This lower surface is pared clean and accurately shaped (Fig 7.13), an inverted shallow gouge being used to round the sharp corner of the lower fold. The next layer is done in the same way (Fig 7.14).

FINISHING TOUCHES

When the ends have been completely shaped it is possible to slightly undercut all round, but this was rarely done. Another finishing touch is to pare the edge with a straight-edged chisel, most efficiently a skew chisel, held at 45°. This gives a ribbon edge which emphasizes the pattern and, incidentally, shows up imperfections in your finish.

The appearance of embroidery was an additional embellishment (Fig 7.15). It was created by simple stab cuts and punch work. A V tool or veiner will provide a hem. Other complexities were the use of foliage sprouting from the ends or the addition of chip carving.

FIG 7.11 *Stabbing down the edge of the upper fold. Note that the corner of the gouge does not reach the turn of the fold.*

FIG 7.12 *The top of the second layer is started by cutting in from the corner of the fold with a deep gouge.*

FIG 7.13 *Cutting along the top of the lower fold.*

FIG 7.14 *The edge of the lower fold has been stabbed in the same way as in Fig 7.11. The deep gouge cuts across the corner of the bottom fold. The corners of the folds descend continuously from one level to the next.*

COLOUR AND FINISHES, INCLUDING FUMING

Traditionally these carvings may have been painted (*see* Fig 7.2), but time and changes in fashion make it hard for us to know how much this was done. Surviving examples are mostly in apparently untreated wood or were beeswaxed, oiled or varnished. The colour may be changed by washing the oak with washing soda. This will redden it but will also raise any rough grain. A blacker or greyer brown can be obtained by fuming, which does not raise the grain. The dark oak found in stables as a result of the presence of horses' urine is thought to have suggested the idea of exposing oak to concentrated ammonia fumes. Simply place the panel in a transparent plastic bag. If it is balanced on pins the gas will affect the underside as well. Slide in a saucer full of household ammonia and seal the bag. Obviously this must be done in a well-ventilated place. If it is done early in the day you can watch the colour change and stop the process when the desired shade has been reached.

FIG 7.15 *A piece of linenfold with a stabbed and punched embroidery pattern. A V tool was used to mark the hem. The edge of the material has been chamfered to strengthen it and to make it read clearly. Carved by Rachel Leiby.*

CHAPTER 8

CARVING A COMMONPLACE OBJECT IN HIGH RELIEF

FINDING INTEREST IN THE ORDINARY

There is a natural tendency for us to look for beauty in certain contexts: flowers, landscapes, the human face and figure, animals. There is beauty to be found elsewhere, however, if only we look at commonplace objects with a kindlier eye.

In dealing with the carving of foliage I have indicated that one is bound to simplify or develop shapes, perhaps unconsciously. If someone takes, for instance, a squashed drinks can and enlarges it in another material we can see the shapes in it merely as shapes and forget about its former function and its present status as rubbish. What you make does not have to be beautiful. A shape may be strong but disturbing; it may contain a powerful social, religious or political message. This chapter is concerned with looking at ordinary things, finding interest and perhaps pleasure in them, and transmitting your feelings about them in carved wood. To do this you do not need rarefied sensitivity but merely to observe closely and, where opportunity arises, draw attention to the most interesting shapes.

A TYPICAL SUBJECT: A BANANA

A half-peeled banana is a good subject. We handle it often but seldom see it as other than food. It is difficult not to find good shape here. As with the leaves in Chapters 5 and 6, draw several first to get an understanding of the form. When this banana was placed casually the shapes were good but it was possible to help the skin into a more satisfying composition. Seen from above the forms looked scattered and so a slight adjustment was made to the stem end until the banana fitted into an elliptical space. This adjustment is in no way false to the spirit of the banana. It still looks natural (Fig 8.1).

MAKING A MODEL AND CHOOSING THE WOOD

Obviously a banana would not keep its shape for more than a day or two once the skin was opened, so a Plasticine model was made (Fig 8.2). Then a piece of wood was selected which would fit the shape. In this case it was decided to make the carving about the same size as the original. As the purpose is to make a carving and not an exact replica of a banana it is not important to match the colour of the wood with that of the original. Indeed, by using another colour of wood it should be possible to draw attention to the shapes more powerfully. If it is too like the real banana viewers may simply say, 'How clever!' and move on, not having experienced any of the carver's excitement about the shapes. The wood used here is a piece of slightly spalted apple. It might have been better if the wood had been sound as the spalting has put straight lines into the timber. The figure of the rest, however, is subdued and so does not give contradictory messages to the curves of the banana. Other reasons for choosing apple were its close-grained texture and firmness, and it was available. An open-grained piece of oak or ash, for instance, would not only have had a disturbing figure but would also have been more difficult to handle in the thin edges. The darkness or lightness of the wood is also important.

LIGHT VERSUS DARK WOOD

A shape like the banana needs shadows to make it fully understood. Shadows would get lost in a dark wood such as laburnum, walnut or mahogany. Many carvers automatically choose lime. Indeed, here, it would show up shadows, have no contradictory figure and be suitable for

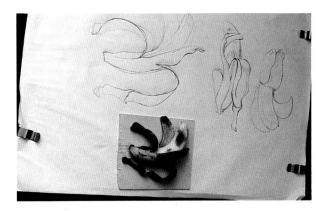

FIG 8.1 *A banana with its skin arranged into a balanced composition by Howard Spiers, preparatory to carving.*

FIG 8.2 *The drawn plan view with a Plasticine model from which the carver can work. Both drawing and modelling help to fix the shape in his mind and thus speed the carving.*

the detail, but is a lustreless wood. Sycamore, which when seasoned is both hard and tough, and birch, which tends to be brittle, would have the advantage of an inner glow, a lustrous quality in the cell walls. In fact any wood, not too dark, even-textured, and without a strong directional pattern would do.

TO CARVE IN THE ROUND OR IN RELIEF?

While it would be possible to carve this banana as a free-standing form the skin would have so much short grain that it would be tempting fate even if it survived the carving. Stood on its end it would be unnatural. The obvious treatment is to carve it in high relief, in which case it needs to be kept attached to the ground, not an easy thing to do if it is not to look as though it is sinking into a soft substance.

ROUGHING OUT

Having done some drawings, made a model and chosen the wood, the next step is to mark the depth of the ground on the wood. With this piece it was possible to saw down the corners to above the ground line and split off much waste quickly (Figs 8.3, 8.4).

As explained with the Chapter 5 leaf, the two best ways for a novice to set down are to start by running a V tool or deep gouge around the outline or by stabbing down about 2mm (⅛in) outside

FIG 8.3 *The drawing transferred to the surface of the wood and the ground line established. The corners were quickly removed by saw cuts.*

the drawn line using the mallet. In both cases care should be taken to prevent the wood from splitting into the area of the design. After this stage the procedure is the same. With a deep gouge cuts are made horizontally across the grain towards the side of what will be the banana. Because both methods of setting down leave an aura of waste wood all around there is no fear of cutting in too far. The wood's splitting quality can be used to your advantage, as described in Chapter 5.

With a piece this deep the ground will be taken down in several stages. Approach the carving methodically by going from one end to the other to create one level and then returning to do the next, which should accelerate the process. If you have plenty of experience or if you are confident about drawing on an uneven surface, you could save time by taking the top surface down where you know it is low, before drawing in and cutting up to the outline. Once the background has been reduced to a corrugated surface virtually at the final depth, it can be levelled with a flattish gouge (No. 3, 4 or 5) and the outline can be cut closely. It does not matter if cuts go too deeply at this stage as the background can be taken a little lower at the end. Areas which are surrounded or difficult to reach into because of the direction of the grain may be tackled with a spoon bit, followed by a nearly flat grounder.

ESTABLISHING HIGHS AND LOWS

Once the outline is accurately cut it is safe to establish which are the high and the low areas, sloping the wood from one to the other where appropriate. It is best not to isolate forms exactly. Either stab down a little way out from the outlines as before or, more safely, run around them with a deep gouge or V tool. Figures 8.5 and 8.6 show two stages in setting down.

Howard Spiers, the student who carved this and several other examples in these chapters, set down

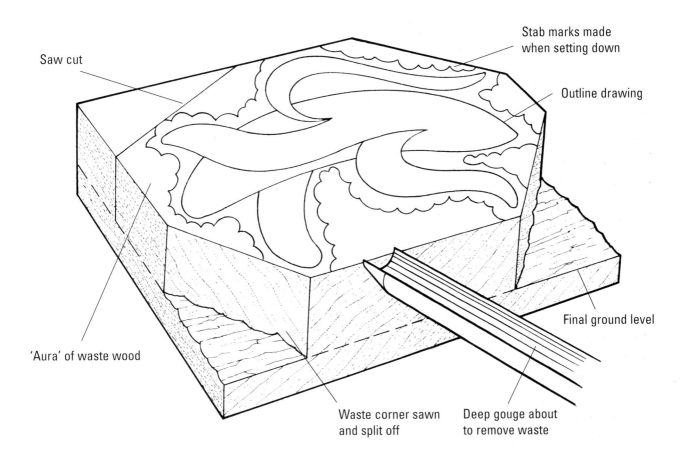

FIG 8.4 *Stages in setting down the outline once the corners have been sawn and split off.*

FIG 8.5 *An early stage in setting down.*

FIG 8.6 *The outline has been set down and the lowest levels established.*

the ground then began creating the relative high and low points only to discover that he needed to go far deeper. He had come up against two natural tendencies to beware of: one is to be conservative about how much we take away; the other is to tend to flatten forms.

BEGINNING THE MODELLING

Whenever one is uncertain about where to begin the modelling (shaping) of a form, it is always a good idea to separate forms which cross over each other. In this case the banana skin crosses over the flesh on top and there is the piece of skin which lies almost flat on the ground (Figs 8.7, 8.8). Once these have been approximately carved one can set about shaping the flesh part and carving the flattish panels of the skin where they still cover the core (Fig 8.9). However tempting it may be it is extremely risky, and unnecessary on this carving, to undercut any part until the forms are complete (Fig 8.10).

How the wood is cut is very much up to the carver. Carving along the grain with broad flattish gouges (Nos. 2 [Swiss] to 5, about 18mm [¾in] or 25mm [1in] wide) gives strong planes, burnishes

the wood and makes a good surface for drawing on. Carving around the forms, going across the grain with a No. 8, 9, 10 or 11 makes for deeper modelling of the forms. Provided that the corners of the chisel do not get under the surface of the wood there is less likelihood of splitting – unless this is intended. You are more in command of the shape. A gouge 12mm (½in) wide should be sufficient here, although if the wood is soft enough and you have the strength a bigger one will be faster but not able to enter narrow regions. A broad, flat one can then be used to smooth the surface for redrawing the final details.

UNDERCUTTING A CYLINDRICAL FORM

The undercutting effectively begins when the banana is rounded underneath, but it is not safe to do this until the top forms and sides are more or less carved to size. Undercutting of a rounded form poses problems. If you carve a cylinder on a flat surface it will touch along only a very narrow line. The danger is that you could miscalculate and separate the round form from its background. You may avoid the danger by going too far the other

FIG 8.7 *Beginning the modelling.*

FIG 8.8 *The skin over the flesh has been modelled further and the flower end of the fruit is pinched in.*

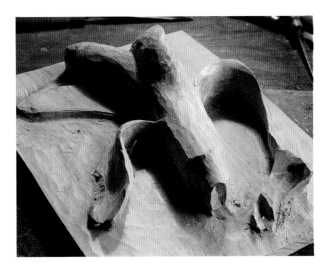

FIG 8.9 *The skin is more defined. Some undercutting of the skin has been done as its shape is now clear.*

FIG 8.10 *The undercutting of the overhanging piece of skin is not attempted until the flesh part has been shaped.*

way and make it look as if the carved object is partially submerged in the ground. If you look carefully there may appear slight gaps between the banana and the ground. The carver must decide whether any gap is useful, whether it helps one to read the form and whether the gap is a good shape. Usually a tiny gap is not helpful and is not particularly pleasing. It may also reveal that the surfaces on opposite sides are not in line, which could be disastrous. At all times while carving you must remember that you are not working with the same materials as the banana is made from. You are making something far more useful and stimulating than a replica. If a replica is what you want you should make a mould and take a cast, but a carving in wood is altogether different. It is a combination of the carver's interpretation of a banana and his technical ability. Viewers automatically accept the limitation of carved wood, so if you tread a middle path between undercutting too far and not undercutting enough the shapes will look convincing. The safe and successful approach is to carve the bottom shape inwards so that it does not form a complete circle

but the last bit where it tucks under should turn very quickly to create a deep shadow (Fig 8.11).

HOW MUCH DETAIL TO SHOW

It is entirely up to the carver how much detail is put into the surface. It is very important not to confuse texture with form. The major grooves on the sides of the banana flesh, for instance, are not just grooves; they are caused by the dipping in of the surface. This important consideration when dealing with veins on leaves and creases on human and other forms deserves emphasis (Fig 8.12). Figures 8.13 and 8.14 show a V chisel carving a groove and an inverted shallow gouge rounding the form into it.

My interest in carving is in the forms and not the surface. Some may prefer to copy exactly the minute transverse ridging of the flesh and the inside of the skin, but obviously you have to stop somewhere. If the surface is left with shallow chisel marks (Fig 8.15) it will have a softer effect and hold the eye better than one that is sanded very smooth, particularly one treated with a shiny

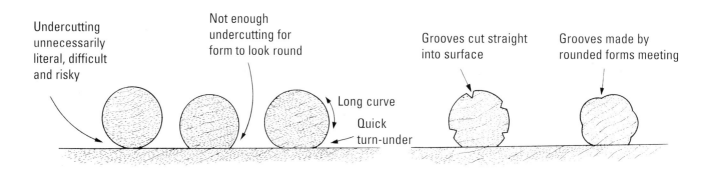

FIG 8.11 *Undercutting a cylindrical form on a flat surface.*

FIG 8.12 *Grooves as slashes and as junctions between forms.*

FIG 8.13 *Marking a groove with a V chisel.*

FIG 8.14 *Rounding the surface of the banana down to the bottom of the groove with an inverted gouge.*

finish. Conversely, if every detail of the surface is carved or worked in with punches or other tools there is a danger that the surface is all that the viewer sees.

The surfaces of the banana flesh and the inside of the skin are marked with both lengthwise and transverse patterns. The longitudinal ones are stronger, so if any surface texture is to be attempted these long grooves and ridges are the most that should be cut. The sensible way to treat

the pattern is merely to cut along the form with a shallow gouge or even a straight-edge on the convex surfaces such as the banana flesh. The slight ridges emphasize the direction of the form and its movement.

EXPLOITING THE EDGES

The treatment of the edges of the banana skin may also be used to suggest movement by cutting

FIG 8.15 *Texturing the inside of the skin.*

FIG 8.16 *Creating a ribbon edge to the skin.*

them down to a thin ribbon at right angles to the surfaces. This changes direction as the surface tilts one way or the other. A skew chisel chases the edges easily (Fig 8.16).

SMOOTHING THE OUTSIDE OF THE BANANA

The outside of the banana skin and the ground both need a broader treatment. It may be possible to give the slight roundness of the outside of the skin by using a broad nearly flat gouge (Swiss No. 2 or 3, English No. 3 or 4) with the flute side face down to the wood (Fig 8.17). An inside bevel will help here. An equivalent degree of sweep on a backbent would also do. The cutting edge should be broad enough for both corners to stay out of the wood. On an inside curve it is impossible to carve with the grain all the way. At some point the edge will get under the grain and the wood will have to be cut from the opposite direction. If you are going to leave a chiselled finish the only way – unless you are incredibly lucky in getting the opposing cuts to meet – is to cut across the grain at this junction with the shallowest gouge that will fit

the curve while keeping its corners out of the grain (Fig 8.18).

FINISHES

Sandpapering away blemishes, repeating the process through the grades of papers to flour paper (about 400 grit) makes a really smooth surface that can look more like plastic than wood. With practice a chiselled finish is quicker and leaves crisper, more lively forms. If there are any slight roughnesses they may be removed with a quick rubbing with flour paper at the very end.

Whether to use oil or wax here depends a little on the wood. Linseed oil darkens and may lose some of the shadows. It is also inclined to look rather muddy on lime and pine. Tung and Danish oil are barely more successful. Sanding sealer will possibly raise the grain and require sandpapering. Sandpaper then will skate over the rims of chisel cuts, leaving the hollows dark and furry. In any case, the use of sanding sealer before wax or oil is quite unnecessary and thickens the surface. A clear wax used sparingly on its own leaves the wood more or less its original colour and tends to pull the surface together (Fig 8.19). If it is too shiny it can be rubbed down with white spirit or 0000 grade steel. However, steel

FIG 8.17 *Smoothing the outside of the skin.*

FIG 8.18 *Cutting across the grain where its direction changes.*

wool should be avoided if there are nibs left on the wood which might catch it.

CHOOSING A SIMILAR SUBJECT TO CARVE YOURSELF

The banana has been used here simply as an example. Of course it may be copied, but the greatest reward lies in choosing your own subject. Choose a subject with a strong but irregular shape. More intricate carvings may tempt the inexperienced, but plenty of practice on simple subjects first is more rewarding in the end.

FIG 8.19 *The carving finished with wax.*

CHAPTER 9

CARVING IN THE ROUND

The two most common blocks which I encounter with students are convictions that they are not artistic and that they cannot draw. Although this book is mainly concerned with techniques I hope incidentally to dispel these beliefs.

THE VIRTUAL IMPOSSIBILITY OF NOT BEING ARTISTIC

Unless you work like a pattern-maker, whenever you carve an object you put something of yourself into it and thereby enter, if only a little way, into the realm of art. Choice of subject and treatment also come into art and that is why most of the examples in this book are used as demonstrations of approach and technique, not as patterns to be closely followed.

DRAWING AS A TOOL

I have earlier written about the need to draw and that a carver should be aiming not so much at making a good picture as learning how forms behave by the concentrated study that drawing provides. You could, of course, learn as much by modelling or carving the object but that is very slow. Besides, you need a means of recording visual images, whether from the outside world or from your imagination, when you have no access to modelling or carving equipment. It is visual note-taking.

My purposes in this chapter are to deal with the problems of carving simple forms in the round and, as a means to making them, some of the ways of conveying depth in drawings.

DRAWING LINES

First, I wish to consider the qualities lines can have. An excellent way of developing control and confidence is to draw innumerable lines with long strokes holding a soft pencil or piece of charcoal at arm's length, working with both hands unsupported. A roll of wall lining paper is not expensive and can be pulled over a drawing board

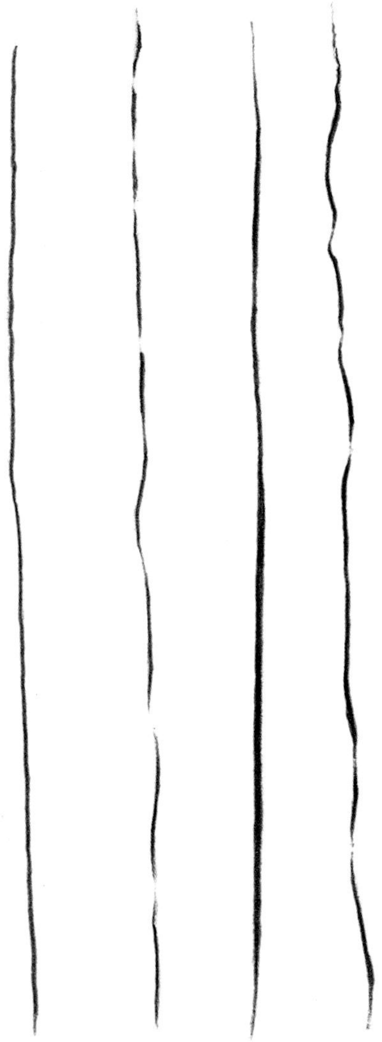

FIG 9.1 *Various lines. The one on the left lacks interest.*

FIG 9.2 *A quick sketch without worrying about completing all the lines.*

as it gets used up. Try drawing lines vertically, horizontally, diagonally, and in waves and circles. Vary the pressure, twisting the drawing implement so that the stroke changes from thick to thin, letting the stick or pencil wobble or skip over the surface to make an irregular line (Fig 9.1).

You will notice that a line drawn with even pressure from end to end looks as lifeless as a piece of wire compared with a line that tapers, wiggles or skips. What happens is that the eye travels along it at the same speed, while a varying line

takes the eye along a more exciting course as it stops, starts, wanders or accelerates. Practising for ten or so minutes daily will eventually develop your confidence and judgement of what makes a good line while your physical control grows to match.

Try drawing an outline, varying the quality of the line. This can easily be done by concentrating less on the precise direction than on the overall pattern (Fig 9.2). Do not press hard or your line will look deliberate and heavy.

CONVEYING A SENSE OF DEPTH

If you are drawing with a view to making something in the round you need to indicate how the forms advance and retreat in depth (Fig 9.3). There are various means of doing this. One of them is perspective, a theory which explains the fact that things further away appear to be smaller and, depending on whether the viewer is looking down on these or up from below, move up or down the picture plane. If the viewer is also looking slightly from the side even more clues can be observed (Fig 9.4). But if you wish to indicate depth in a sphere it is much harder unless it has lines on it as on a geographical globe (Fig 9.5) or applies the following principles.

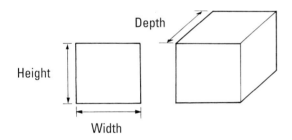

FIG 9.3 *The three dimensions.*

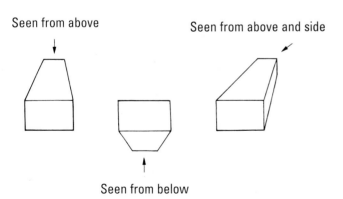

Seen from above

Seen from above and side

Seen from below

FIG 9.4 *Perspective.*

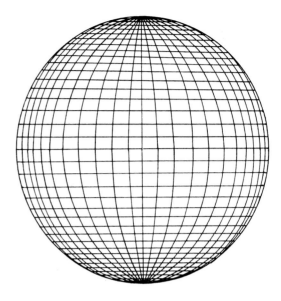

FIG 9.5 *Using the principle of lines getting closer together as they go round a curve.*

As well as things appearing smaller with smaller intervals between them the further away they are, they also lose definition of detail and become less strongly contrasted. A view of countryside on an ordinarily humid day will show strong contrasts of light and shade in the foreground and fainter outlines far away, as in ranges of hills (Fig 9.6).

The contrast between a very dark line or patch of shadow with the white of your paper makes it jump forward in the same way (Fig 9.7).

USING LIGHTING TO CONVEY DEPTH

To portray depth and to record information a carver or sculptor has to show not only what is seen but what is known to be there. Lighting can cause problems. If you have several light sources they create conflicting shadows which destroy the illusion of depth in a form when drawn. I prefer to eliminate from my mind all but one light source when drawing, or if possible place an object I wish to draw so that it is lit from one direction only. This means everything facing towards the light is white and everything furthest from the light is darkest with varying depths of shade on other surfaces. A sphere shows this well (Fig 9.8).

The danger with A is that the strong contrast of the shadow with the white paper makes that edge jump forward. B is safer and follows the rule that parts further away are less strongly shaded. The use of cast shadow in C also helps, although if it crosses a part of another form it can hide important detail. Note that without the lighter shadow on the underside of the sphere the cast shadow would appear as part of the form.

METHODS OF SHADING

Shading can be done by various methods.

1 Toning: simply varying the intensity of tone by changing density and pressure of strokes (*see* Fig 9.8).

2 Stippling: where the dots are closer together the shadow is deeper (Fig 9.9A).
3 Cross-hatching (Fig 9.9B).
4 Describing the shape by running the pencil around it and making the lines denser where the shadows fall strongly (Fig 9.9C).

It is important with these methods that you are consistent in your viewpoint (Fig 9.10).

TWO EXAMPLES OF CARVING COMMONPLACE OBJECTS IN THE ROUND

A DENTED DRINKS CAN

When carving a squeezed drinks can Howard Spiers did his first drawings putting in all the shadows he saw. After eliminating all but one major light source the results are markedly more intelligible in three dimensions (Figs 9.11, 9.12).

The carving itself, as usual, involved selection of timber, in this case a piece of oak fence post, and deciding how to hold it. As far as possible I try to

FIG 9.6 *Stronger contrasts in the foreground.*

FIG 9.7 *Drawing using dark and faint lines.*

A
Heavy shading on outside

B
Heaviest shading fades towards edge

C
Cast shadow hides the small sphere

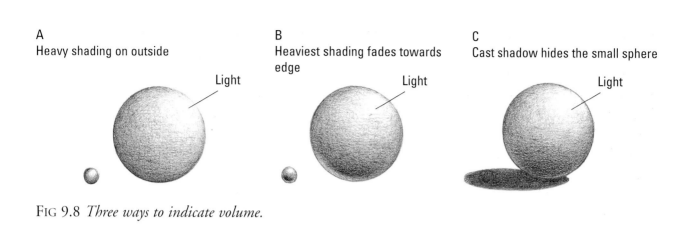

Light

Light

Light

FIG 9.8 *Three ways to indicate volume.*

A
Stippling

B
Hatching

C
Contour shading

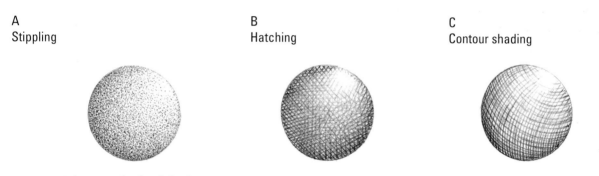

FIG 9.9 *Three methods of shading.*

Consistent shading with contour lines

Inconsistent contour shading

Looking into a curved cylinder

Looking into a bent cylinder

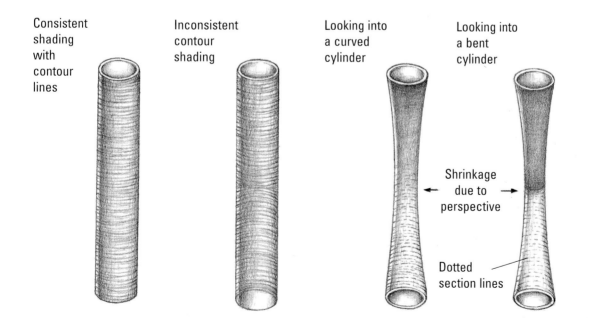

Shrinkage due to perspective

Dotted section lines

FIG 9.10 *Using shading consistently.*

FIG 9.11 *Preparatory drawing of a squashed drinks can by Howard Spiers. This drawing is not intelligible as a three-dimensional representation.*

FIG 9.13 *Top view of the can at an early stage.*

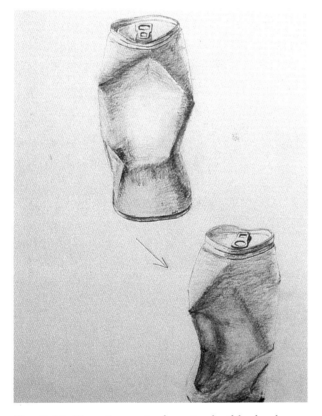

FIG 9.12 *Drawing revised to give legible depth. The arrow shows the direction of the light.*

FIG 9.14 *Side view of the can at an early stage. Note the square block left for holding on the bench.*

leave a piece of the wood which can be sacrificed at or near the finish or be turned into a base. It is best if it is square so that if it is rotated the vice needs only minor movement each time. If you need to carve the whole block and the underneath of the finished piece will not be seen, the work can be held by a bench screw or screwed to a square block or a universal vice.

The form was basically cylindrical and so the first task was to make it round, starting with the top. Carving a sculpture out of a cylindrical piece of wood can be difficult, as it is sometimes hard to remember where you were standing when you drew any line on it. In this case, the major dents were on opposite sides of the can so it was not too difficult to establish the major planes. As with the reliefs in earlier chapters, control is greater if you carve across the grain with a deep gouge, but it is possible to cut out major shapes with saws. The main thing here is not to cut too close to the finished shape – about 12mm (½in) is a reasonable amount of waste to leave on a piece of this size. You could also cut large planes with a broad, flat

FIG 9.15 *The finished carving with the original can painted grey to help the forms to be read.*

chisel or gouge along the grain. Saw cuts across the grain into large indentations make this easier. Each method will work and will produce slightly different results. After removing large pieces with a saw I prefer carving around the form (Figs 9.13, 9.14). A major advantage is that a flat or square look is less likely. It is worth keeping the offcuts as they can then be used for something else or kept in case they are needed for patching if things go wrong. Figure 9.15 shows the finished carving.

A TAP ON A COLUMN OF WATER

The other carved example here is one I had in mind for some time (Fig 9.16). The movement of water is essentially a thing of change. It cannot be copied so it demands stylization. The column of water and the pool it splashes into would make a sculpture in its own right but I felt that the regular shape of the tap, apart from the context that it provides, sets off the haphazard flow of the water. I have not striven for literal representation of a tap. Since it has only to look right no great care was taken with measurements. The water was represented by shapes generally associated with water movement: ripples, droplets, spiralling forms which separate and merge and random bubbles and waves.

Anticipating Future Breakage of Short Grain

The bulk of the waste wood was band-sawn off and kept (Fig 9.17). Being fragile and furthest from the held end, the tap was carved first. The stem was carved around the grain with a deep gouge (Fig 9.18). It was then made regular with a riffler (Fig 9.19) and finished with a flat gouge.

I then made the water column approximately cylindrical. Using my drawing and a clay maquette (*see* Fig 9.16) as guides but allowing the tools and the wood some part in the design, I first marked the main forms with a 60° V tool

(Fig 9.20) but could have stabbed them in with a variety of flattish gouges. This method was used later to give deeper shadows with sharp depths (Fig 9.21). Droplets were formed by using No. 7 or 8 gouges with the flute downwards or with backbent gouges (Fig 9.22). If you do not have inside bevels or if you are carving tight inside curves, backbent tools are essential for quick and tidy carving of this sort of shape.

To shape the concave grooves under the splash two spoonbit gouges were used: a broad, shallow one to make the overall shape and a 10mm (⅜in) one with a No. 9 sweep for the detail (Fig 9.23). Using various smaller ones and bent V tools would have added to the range of shapes.

Building up by Lamination

The pool of water is considerably wider than the tap and so it would be uneconomical to carve the whole sculpture out of one big piece of wood. I could have carved the pool out of another piece of wood, but as I had sufficient off-cuts after band-sawing the front and side profiles it seemed sensible to build up the bottom with those. Normally when laminating timber I arrange for the annual rings to be opposed so the shrinkage pulls in different directions (Fig 9.24). However, the piece of 100mm x 50mm (4in x 2in) American red oak chosen for this carving was virtually quarter-sawn and well seasoned. It was therefore fairly stable and would allow for the blocks to be placed with the annual rings all curving more or less in the same direction. This meant that the pool was to be carved into end grain but practice had shown that the wood when carved in this direction, although being slightly brittle and crumbly, would take fine detail. To allow access to the bottom of the water column and the splash the lamination was left until those parts were done.

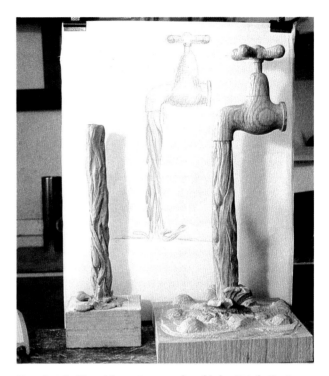

FIG 9.16 *Tap (American red oak) by Dick Onians. From the left: Plasticine model of a column of water, the original drawing and finished carving.*

FIG 9.17 *The shape bandsawn to yield large offcuts.*

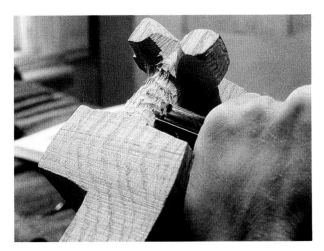

FIG 9.18 *Carving around the body of the tap with a deep gouge.*

FIG 9.19 *Using a riffler to shape the stem of the tap.*

FIG 9.20 *A V tool marking out the elements in the water flow.*

FIG 9.21 *Using a chip carving technique to deepen grooves and define shapes.*

Before lamination the pieces were arranged to give the best grain pattern and marked underneath. When joining timber it is easiest to glue one plane at a time so I squared the front and back ends of the pieces and glued them so that I extended the base in front of and behind the water column and had two matching side pieces. When the adhesive was set I planed the sides to fit tightly and assembled the whole bottom (Fig 9.25). Glue lines are distracting so should be as fine as possible. If a hard glue like Cascamite is used thick glue lines will also rapidly blunt the tools. I used PVA (the common white liquid wood adhesive). The bubbles were then roughed out with a 12mm

(½in) No. 11 gouge carving across the grain (Fig 9.26). The tap handles were short-grained, so to reduce the chance of accidental breakage in the future they were broken and reinforced with bamboo dowel (Figs 9.27, 9.28).

THE SHAPE OF THE BASE

When the carving was finished I could have made the base circular or oval, as this tends to lead the eye around the sculpture and prevents it from having any obvious front, back and sides. As a tap conventionally has these views anyway, it seemed sensible to leave the base square.

FIG 9.22 *A backbent gouge making the droplets convex.*

FIG 9.23 *Shaping grooves under the splash with a deep spoon bit gouge.*

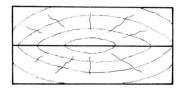

FIG 9.24 *Usual ways of arranging grain for lamination.*

Cupping towards the outside of the tree

The dotted line shows the board cupped after drying

FIG 9.25 *The carving is completed to the bottom of the splash before adding the wood for the pool of water. The pieces on each side are both made up of laminated offcuts.*

FIG 9.26 *Roughing out the bubbles with a No. 11 gouge.*

FIG 9.27 *The handles of the tap were broken and dowelled for strength.*

FIG 9.28 *The handles were glued and held with a cam clamp which is both light and gentle.*

THE FINISH

Since the grain is strongly marked I tested scrap pieces with linseed and Danish oils and Briwax and Renaissance Wax to discover the appropriate finish. I decided upon one coat of Danish oil as it was not too shiny, did not make the grain distracting and it emphasized the shadows.

Danish oil contains tung oil, a natural oil from a tree found in China. It is thinner and faster drying than tung oil. They are both water resistant. Briwax is a proprietary brand which is basically beeswax but also contains carnauba wax and other unspecified ingredients. It can be bought as clear and in several colours. It gives a hard and bright shine. Renaissance Wax is a proprietary brand of microcrystalline wax. It is very soft, leaves no noticeable colour in the wood and imparts only a slight sheen. It protects the surface of the wood and can even clean a dirty wax or varnish finish.

CHAPTER 10

CARVING
A BOWL

A bowl is not only a useful receptacle; it is a sculpture, too. It offers wonderful opportunities to the carver for abstract or representational design, and for the beginner teaches an enormous amount about designing, choice of wood, methods of holding and carving work in the round.

FINDING INSPIRATION AND MAKING THE DESIGN

Sometimes the design may be suggested by the shape of a piece of wood; sometimes it is the result of considerable planning.

A bowl is a receptacle deeper than a plate but may be any shape or size. This means it may have an uneven rim (Figs 10.1, 10.2). It may also have holes in it. It may have a simple shape with surface decoration (Fig 10.3). It should continue to stand firmly when things are put in it.

Bowls fail for one or more of the following reasons: because the shape is poor; the wood splits during carving or in use; it is impossible to hold it steady in the making; the appearance of the grain is not fully exploited; the direction of the grain makes the carving needlessly difficult; the carver makes the bowl disastrously thin through carelessness or through some nasty trick played by the wood. Most of these faults arise from lack of planning.

Inspiration may come directly from nature, for example from leaf, nut and shell forms. If these

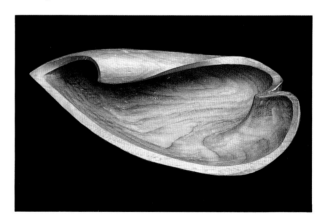

FIG 10.1 *Bowl in walnut with uneven edge (Dick Onians).*

FIG 10.2 *Bowl in 'olive' ash with heartwood at bottom and varying thicknesses of rim (Dick Onians).*

FIG 10.3 *Kashmiri bowl with surface decoration in Kashmir walnut.*

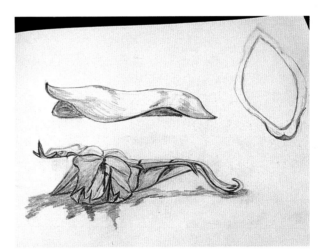

FIG 10.4 *Leaf drawings as inspiration for bowl (Howard Spiers).*

are to be used I refer to my advice in previous chapters about learning the forms by much drawing. The subject may then be drawn or modelled from memory and adapted to bowl form. This may only involve flattening the base so that it sits well. It may, however, involve a degree of simplification or even abstraction from the original source (Figs 10.4, 10.5, 10.6). The possibilities are boundless.

If you wish to invent your own abstract shape I would refer you to Chapter 14 on Carving an Abstract. As this is a risky area it is helpful to make a series of clay or Plasticine models and experiment until you are convinced about the design. The rim need not be all the same width;

indeed varying the thickness makes for greater interest and speeds the eye around (Fig 10.7). Nor need the rim all face in the same direction. Contrasts of rounded hollows in angular blocks or vice versa can also be pleasing (Fig 10.8).

Whether the bowl is completely abstract or derived more or less closely from nature I recommend that the object be considered as a whole, having a deliberate pattern or rhythm (Figs 10.7, 10.9), different views all suggesting the same form.

FIG 10.5 *Plasticine model and bowl begun by Howard Spiers in beech. Note the lug at the left end for holding.*

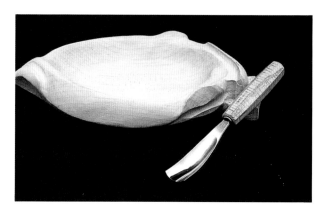

FIG 10.6 *Beech bowl nearly finished, showing a No. 8 long-bend gouge resting against the holding lug which is still retained.*

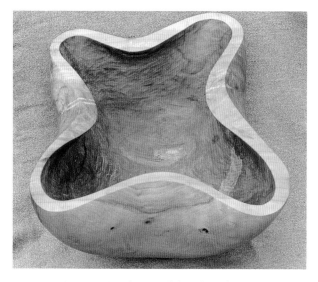

FIG 10.7 *Large apple-wood bowl with rhythmic rim of varying thicknesses (Dick Onians).*

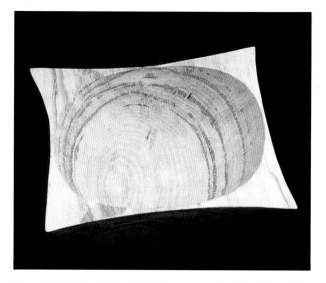

FIG 10.8 *Beech bowl with contrasting inside and outside shapes (Dick Onians).*

FIG 10.9 *Leaf-inspired bowl in spalted ash using echoing curves (Dick Onians).*

FIG 10.10 *Large birch burr bowl (Dick Onians).*

TAKING INSPIRATION FROM THE SHAPE OF THE WOOD

Sometimes a burr or an irregularly shaped piece of wood suggests a bowl (Fig 10.10). A burr usually makes the form of the bowl clear but a weird or suggestive shape in a piece of wood may entice you into beginning a sculpture which works well from all but one or two views. It will need special care in the planning. Burrs and irregular pieces may also contain dead knots, inclusions of bark and internal shakes. The grain, too, is unpredictable, and more wood may split away than one expects.

SELECTING THE PIECE OF WOOD

Where the wood does not suggest the shape but the design comes first, the wood needs careful selection. If the bowl is to be thin all around then it may be carved in green wood provided it is done quickly. There is so little wood left that even if the wood does move the whole shape distorts rather than splits. This means that tough timbers such as beech, ash and sycamore, hard to carve when seasoned but easy when green, are suitable. It is tempting to look at a log split or sawn down the middle and see the curved outside of a bowl already there.

There are pitfalls here: the sapwood of timber is the least durable and attractive part, yet the sides and bottom of a bowl carved from a half-log in this way are mainly sapwood; heartshakes too tend to develop in the rim at each end. Well-seasoned timber should be safe. If the bowl is taken from quarter-sawn timber without the heart in it, it will probably be stable, but the figure may appear mainly as stripes, usually darker on the heartwood side. An excellent method, although it does make for a smaller bowl

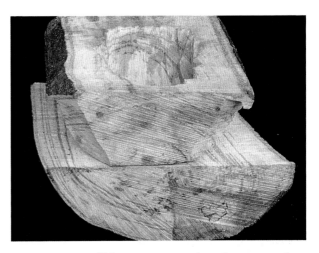

FIG 10.11 *Half-logs repositioned as they grew; the bowl is being carved with heartwood running along the base to eliminate most of the sapwood. This piece of beech has interesting drought stress marks.* (See also *Fig 10.8.*)

and greater waste, is to use a half-log with the heart running through the base of the bowl (Figs 10.2, 10.11). Parts of the rim will probably have sapwood in them but the better colour and figure will cover a larger area.

A bowl may have the grain running vertically. This makes for difficulties in carving since much of the cutting is against the grain and there is great risk of shakes in unseasoned wood. However, when a bowl is successfully made out of a round sawn out of a log the annual rings can be very striking.

RELATION BETWEEN AVAILABLE TOOLS AND SIZE OF BOWL

The size of the bowl depends on the available timber, your purpose in making the bowl and your tools. A chain saw and an angle grinder with a special wood-carving disc make really big bowls feasible and ease cutting down against the grain if it is vertical. Their size affects the size of the bowl (Figs 10.12, 10.20). Both chain saw

FIG 10.12 *The array of tools used for carving the inside of the large sycamore bowl shown in Figure 10.20.*

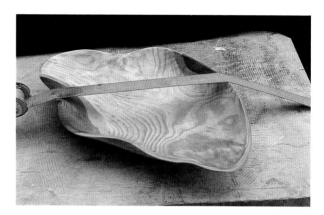

FIG 10.13 *Bowl in Scots pine held by a webbing clamp (Dick Onians). The shape was dictated by the odd shape of the piece.*

and cutting disc are dangerous. They can also run away with you and take out more than intended from the inside, especially near the rim. You need to check frequently that the thickness of the bowl is within sensible limits. Adzes, axes, drills, and hand saws are all possible in the roughing out stages but straight gouges, long bent and spoon bit gouges are essential if you are to be fully in command of the shape. You may be able to get good results with a spoon bit or a long bend alone, but the former is more difficult to control and the latter limits you to shallow bowls. Even rotary burrs and sanders can be too greedy. They will certainly leave a different texture.

HOLDING THE BOWL WHILE CARVING

Before tackling the problem of whether to carve the hollow or the outside of the bowl first it is sensible to consider how the bowl is to be held at all stages of working. Burrs and other extraordinary pieces of wood, being already rounded underneath, pose special problems. I have found webbing clamps useful with these (Fig 10.13), particularly if the wood is cushioned

underneath. If the base is very broad and the sides are steep a clamp or holdfast may reach sufficiently far across the bowl to hold it steady (Fig 10.14). When the hollow is complete a block of wood resting on a soft pad inside the bowl will give purchase for a clamp or holdfast (Fig 10.15). Sometimes a more spreading bowl may be clamped or held in a vice by a strong bar laid across the bowl pressing down on the rim. The lip has to be stout enough for this (Fig 10.16). If the base is to be thick enough a block may be screwed on to the base, which should be flattened first (Fig 10.17). This may be held in a vice or clamped to the bench. In Figure 10.18 the work piece is held in the vice by a block screwed on to its top surface. The length of the screws and their position must be constantly remembered. The base of this example is a mirror image of the leaf forming the bowl and therefore thick (Fig 10.19). An excellent method is to leave a piece of wood at each end which is flat and can be held, preferably by two clamps (Fig 10.20). As the carving approaches completion these platforms are reduced to enable the shape to be completed. Once the bowl is rounded and thin it is difficult and risky to squeeze it in the vice.

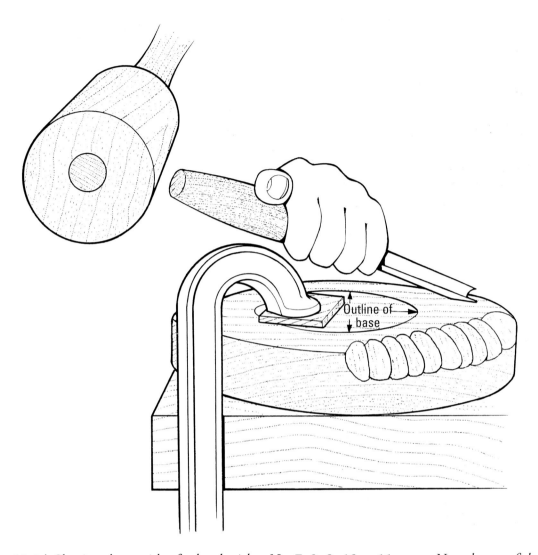

Outline of base

FIG 10.14 *Shaping the outside of a bowl with a No. 7, 8, 9, 10 or 11 gouge. Note the use of the clamp.*

ORDER OF CARVING – INSIDE OR OUTSIDE FIRST?

The decision whether to start with the inside or the outside shape is not to be taken lightly, but it is generally better to shape the outside first. If the shape appears displeasing or something goes wrong the bowl can always be shrunk. If the inside is done first and something goes wrong on the outside the bowl may end up an ugly shape, or too thin or even fail altogether.

If the top of the bowl is uneven at this stage it may be difficult to clamp the bowl upside down, so if possible make it flat and vary it later when carving the inside. First the plan view of the bowl must be cut out, allowing for holding lugs at each end if desired. The shape of the base should then be drawn on.

Start by carving away the corners all round (*see* Fig 10.14), then round again working back towards the base outline. Flatter gouges may get under the grain and split off more than is desired. I recommend gouges from No. 7 upwards. If the chisel has a low cutting angle it is not hard to cut

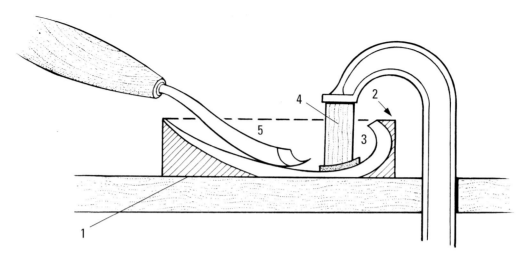

1 Base flattened before beginning carving.

2 Where the side curves out from the lip it is carved downwards.

3 This part is hollowed out first.

4 Block shaped to take the clamp. Leather, card or other packing protects the inside of the bowl.

5 The rest of the inside hollowed out.

6 Carving of the underside.

7 Packing protecting the base from the clamp.

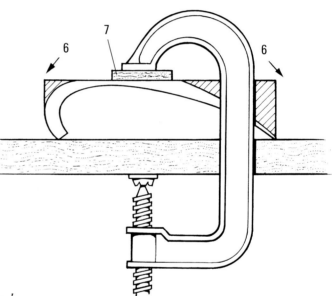

FIG 10.15 *Methods of clamping a hollow bowl.*

downwards, creating the curve of the side towards the rim. If, however, the bowl tapers in to the mouth the side should be carved down from the lip at least some of the way. The wood may be held edge on in the vice and shaped with chisels, rasps or spokeshaves. The last two are easier on the end grain. It is not yet necessary to finish the outside of the bowl. Indeed, any clamping lugs cannot yet be removed.

CARVING THE INSIDE OF THE BOWL

Clamping lugs are particularly useful when the inside is carved, as they allow the clamps to grip firmly without impeding the chisels. The inside of the bowl can be cleared out with whatever tools are available. If doing it entirely by hand a large straight gouge with a deepish sweep (No. 7 up to

FIG 10.16 *The small beech bowl being held in a carver's chops with a bar across its mouth.*

FIG 10.18 *Cherry-wood bowl held in vice by block screwed into top surface of the bowl blank. Note the chisel being used to split off wood to the saw cut.*

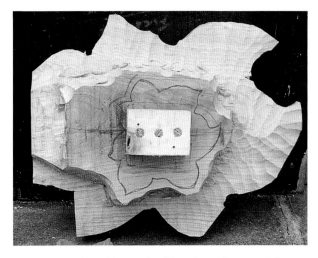

FIG 10.17 *Double ivy leaf bowl in cherry with holding block screwed on base.*

FIG 10.19 *Finished cherry-wood bowl by Roy Taylor.*

No. 11) should be driven in with a scooping motion, working down towards the centre of the bowl but starting well in from the outer edge. This is an occasion when a short, steep, outside bevel gives an advantage. To rapidly establish the depth of the bowl and to make a space for the displaced wood you may drill the centre out, remembering the pilot screw on the end of the drill if it has one. To measure the thickness of the bowl the fingers may provide a reasonable gauge but double-ended callipers are safer.

As the bowl gets deeper enlarge the opening but leave the final inside of the rim until last, as the chisels will bruise it when resting against it. Also avoid catching the shoulder of the chisel or the ferrule on the edge when using the mallet, as that can tear the wood badly. Unless the bowl is very shallow you will need at least one bent gouge. Because of its lower cutting angle a long bent is excellent for applying pressure while maintaining control, but a spoon bit is often needed for the tight curves at the bottoms of bowls (*see* Fig 10.15). Numbers 7, 8 or 9 sweeps are good, but flatter ones may be needed to give a smooth finish. A width of

FIG 10.20 *Large sycamore bowl (Dick Onians) held by lugs deliberately left to reduce obstruction from holding devices.*

19mm (¾in) is a good size. If the lip of the bowl curves inwards the overhang may be difficult to get under. Rotary burrs and sanding drums or flap wheels may help. If you want to leave the whole inside including the overhang straight from the chisel and of an even thickness, the problem of how to finish it should be anticipated in the design stage.

THE FINISH

As the bowl is a sculpture and very much your own design there is nothing to stop you using sandpaper to finish. However, finishing the outside with flat chisels or spokeshave and the inside with gouges fitting as close to the contours as possible will probably do the job faster and leave the cell walls of the wood clearly exposed, not blurred by the effects of paper or rasps. To sandpaper successfully to a fine surface involves painstakingly working down through several grades of paper. You are more likely to get an even surface if the paper is wrapped round a cork block. If the wood is damped between the grades the grain that has been compressed will rise. This is particularly important with softer woods and is essential if a wet finish such as button polish or Danish oil is to be applied as that, too, may make the grain rise and feel rough to handle. Sandpapering away the roughnesses may leave light-coloured marks where there are still high and low spots. Because people will handle bowls and objects will be put in them it is probably wise to soften sharp edges with flour paper but avoid making the edges too rounded or the whole may look lumpy – unless, of course, you wish it to look lumpy. I prefer a finish straight from the chisel as it is quicker, although it also demands greater skill. I then quickly rub it down with flour paper to remove loose whiskers and soften sharp edges before applying an appropriate coating.

A salad bowl should be finished with edible oil but fruit and other bowls may be treated with raw linseed, which imparts a rich, golden colour (not good on lime, however), tung oil or Danish oil, as they are water resistant, or wax. I do not see the need for a sanding sealer before wax. Our ancestors found wax quite good enough on its own. Linseed and wax finishes are marked by water and alcohol. For a French-polished finish the bowl will need to be sanded very finely. Such shellac-based polishes are affected by heat, alcohol and water. Varnishes should be used with care as they may be too shiny and make the bowl look plastic, or may discolour unpleasantly with age.

CHAPTER 11

CARVING AN ANIMAL IN THE ROUND

The twentieth-century carver is at a great disadvantage when carving animals. He has seen too many examples in various media done by sophisticated sculptors to be able to see with a naïve or primitive eye. Being largely a town-dweller he does not spend his life surrounded by animals of the farmyard or countryside. Most experience of animals comes from photographs, films and visits to the zoo.

Early carvers either knew their subjects, but for complex reasons simplified or stylized them, or were trained in a tradition which told them exactly what effects to create and how to make them. Formula carving is the product of workshops all competing for the same work. It has to be done quickly and efficiently. Animals produced this way are stereotyped. Part of the problem for the carver wishing to break away from a set style is the expectation of the clients. These may conservatively demand strict adherence to a style or they may insist on literal accuracy. Try carving a dog breeder's favourite dog!

One of the main themes of this book is that a carver should be more than a model-maker. If carving is to be raised to a level where the carver can express himself freely, honestly and strongly he must go through the process that was achieved by his predecessors over centuries. Unless you are one of the rare carvers with the gift of a strong visual memory you will need to know what it is you are taking liberties with when you stylize or otherwise simplify it.

WHY SOME BEGINNERS FAIL

Some modern amateurs have a poor understanding of animal anatomy and proportion, and their carvings have neither the charm of the primitive nor the conviction of the expert. One view – the one the carver had the photograph of – looks well, but is let down by other views for which he had no information. Meticulous attention may be paid to the surface – feathers, fur, scales – but, although this is often superbly done, it does not disguise the poor modelling of the skeleton and muscles underneath. I have seen bird carvings looking like feather dusters and square dogs with minutely detailed fur.

THE ASPECT OF THE SUBJECT THAT MOST ATTRACTS

We are attracted to animals for many reasons: their grace, quaintness, power, even, in some, a winsome appearance. Before beginning work we should consider which aspect is most important to us. As carvers we are primarily concerned with shape, that is, with grace, power or simply strong forms. A cow lying in a field is not necessarily graceful but is composed of beautiful forms. Owls and walruses may not be beautiful but have very satisfying shapes. I recommend that you avoid winsome expressions and concentrate on shape and line. The basic structure is far more important than surface details. However, if you can hold a feeling of the dominant aspect in your mind while carving there is a good chance it will appear in the finished article.

RESEARCHING THE SUBJECT

This chapter is concerned with reproducing the animal fairly accurately so the first question to ask is whether you know it well enough. If you copy someone else's version you are merely exercising technique. I have noticed that when carvers copy other people's work they tend to emphasize any original mistakes or exaggerations and usually end up with something further from reality than they intended. It is far better to do the research yourself. If all you have is one photograph of a rare animal it is best to forget it unless you can find many other views. If, however, you have access to a collection of

stuffed animals such as the Natural History Museum collection or to a zoo you should visit and take as many photographs as possible and, because photographs seldom give all the information you need, make sketches and diagrams or even take some Plasticine in a box and make a small model. This may entail making a wire armature to act as a frame to support your modelling material. Stuffed animals, however, although they keep still, may have become shrunk or distorted.

STUDYING ANATOMY

There are some people who automatically see the relationship between one part of an animal and another: the way legs join bodies is a good example. But an understanding of what is going on under the surface will make it much easier to model the shape. I recommend a book on animal anatomy such as Ellenberger, Dittrich and Baum's *An Atlas of Animal Anatomy for Artists*, published by Dover, which deals with horse, dog, lion, cow and some other ungulates. An understanding of animal anatomy, easy access to the animal of your choice, preparatory drawings and models give a good chance of success.

Although working like this can lead to academic studies rather than lifelike representations, the chances of later making lively pieces are much improved once you have mastered the forms. This approach may not commend itself to someone seeking instant results, but it does work. Many people now embark on carving in their later years and either have a mental block about drawing or feel that they do not have the time to spend observing when carving is what they want to do. Nevertheless, any drawing is better than none. Get the shape firmly into your head before cutting and the carving will go smoothly. Constantly stopping to consult photographs and anatomy books interrupts the flow, slows you down and makes for stilted work.

DO NOT BE TOO AMBITIOUS

Some beginners have ambitions ahead of their immediate capability. This is not to say that they will not be able to finish their carving eventually, but gaining experience (and tools) while making two or three simpler carvings is a more sensible preliminary. Something which the beginner may take several years to complete could, with experience, be done in a matter of a month or so. You should consider the best use of your time and the risk of frustration at slow progress.

TOO SIMPLE AN APPROACH

Other beginners copy patterns from books and are sometimes content with bandsawing a profile to shape and rounding the forms with rasps. While this is a simple form of sculpture it hardly qualifies as carving, and if done closely to instructions teaches little. The only virtue here is that the rapid result can stimulate the carver on to better things. It is far more rewarding and constructive to carve to your own design some easily seen animal such as a fish, snail or frog, for then you have the thrill of knowing you have done it all yourself.

PUTTING LIFE INTO A POSE

While carving is far easier if the animal's pose is perfectly symmetrical, you could lose on two counts. First, unless the grain is markedly different from one side to the other, a potential for interest is lost as both sides are identical and the back, front and top views are too evenly balanced. Second, such a static pose may contradict your efforts to make the creature seem alive. A turn of the body, head or tail and arrangement of the legs in different positions provides variety and movement. Carving teachers regularly twist their students' clay

maquettes to make them come alive.

A fairly difficult subject such as a quadruped illustrates the problems not only of composition but of timber selection and holding the work.

USING A PATTERN BOOK AND YOUR OWN KNOWLEDGE

The deer shown in this chapter, carved by Howard Spiers, is based on designs in Mary Duke Guldan's excellent *A Woodcarver's Workbook*, published by Fox Chapel and now available from GMC Publications. One thing she does which is missing from many pattern books is to give top views. These provide essential information as well as helping to make a carving read well when viewed all round. Having observed fallow deer in the wild, Howard was well placed to adapt the drawings in the book to this species. He first made careful drawings to fix the shapes in his mind, then selected the wood. You may choose to design the carving to fit a particular piece of wood.

FIG 11.1 *Side view of walnut block showing positioning of deer and first roughing out.*

CHOOSING THE BEST DIRECTION OF THE GRAIN

This carving is in a piece of fast-grown, and therefore fairly tough, walnut. Care has to be taken when positioning the work in the wood. The thin legs demand that the grain run up them rather than across (Fig 11.1). On some animals this may put the nose or tail at risk. Ears generally have to take their chance unless you can insert them without showing a join. Elephants and the few other animals with very short or fat legs are the only ones where the grain can safely run across them. Although wood can be made to be literally as thin as wire or feathers, for instance, if a carving is very fragile its only value is to show the carver's patience and, nowadays, probably his possession of some mechanical detailing tool. The great skill of Grinling Gibbons's style of work was in creating the illusion of fragility while retaining strength. The pose should take account of the wood's limitations.

SELECTING THE FIGURE OF THE WOOD

The pattern of the grain, too, must be considered. Placed with the grain as in Figure 11.2, the convex surfaces on side B will show as concentric rings. On side A there will be vertical stripes. Quarter-sawn wood as in Figure 11.3 will have stripes on both sides. 'Plain sawn' timber, with very much flatter annual rings as in Figure 11.4, will give a good figure on both sides but the wood may 'cup' – not a bad thing if it makes the carving less symmetrical. The fallow deer was carved from technically quarter-sawn wood.

HOLDING THE WOOD

A large square piece is left below the carving to allow it to be held firmly in vice or clamp. This may be converted at the end into the base. The temptation to carve the feet right to the bottom of the block should be avoided. If you want to make

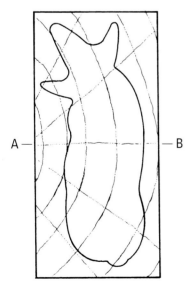

FIG 11.2 *Deeply curved annual rings.*

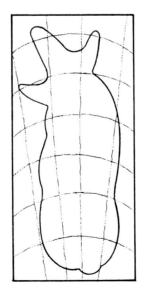

FIG 11.3 *Quarter-sawn.*

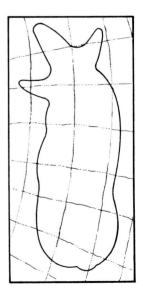

FIG 11.4 *Very flat annual rings.*

FIG 11.5 *Rear view. The saw cuts facilitated removal of large pieces of waste.*

FIG 11.6 *Top view of same stage. The stab marks in the waste wood on the back show how the waste was removed by splitting.*

the carving so big, find another piece of wood. While it is possible to carve the feet to the bottom of the block the task becomes unnecessarily difficult.

BOSTING OUT AND AVOIDING THE SQUARE LOOK

We have all seen square carved birds, animals and people trying to look as if they had the full shape of the natural original. Some primitive carvers tend to work like this, but so much else in their carvings is stylized and their ways of looking and working are so refreshingly different from ours that we respond favourably to the simplicity of their interpretation. Only an experienced artist in our culture can match them. The modern carver's work often looks merely wrong – flat or clumsy. The way we draw things as outlines, the flat view of the world that our eyes transmit to the brain, and our time- and wood-saving methods of preparing the work all

conspire to make flat or square carvings. Sensibly, we cut out the profiles with saws or, if wasting material is not a consideration, with axes or grinding tools. A profile depends entirely on where the viewer is standing, so most beginners take straight front and side views and, if they are wise, top and back views, but are wrong in thinking that it is simply a matter of cutting tightly to these outlines and rounding off the corners. Drawings help to plan these outlines, and models help to reduce the rigidity and put some depth into the forms.

Once the outline has been drawn – in the case of most animals the side view is the one which leads to the removal of the greatest amount of wood most quickly – the waste can be cut away (Figs 11.5, 11.6). Always leave extra wood all the way round. On a piece 150mm (6in) long, about 6mm (¼in) extra is reasonable. The experienced carver may cut closely to the outline but the beginner too often cuts too close in places. Once the drawing has been carved away it is difficult to

FIG 11.7 *Square bear. Front view.*

FIG 11.8 *Square bear. The top view holds a strong memory of the square block it was carved from.*

FIG 11.9 *Playing cats (lime) by Eva Linnemann.*

remember where the mistake happened. The beginner may also fail to eliminate traces of the square block because the profiles are cut at right angles. With a margin for error all around the carver can develop forms if they appear to go wrong.

You must remember that what you have drawn is only a silhouette. In the case of this deer, for instance, the length of the head as it appears in the drawn outline is less than its true length. The right ear occupies more of the silhouette than the left. The tips of the nose and left ear are as close to the side of the block as the left flank.

MORE ABOUT THE SQUARE LOOK

It is true that sometimes a square form can have charm. I illustrate this with an example carved by a student who I believe had copied from drawings in a book (Fig 11.7). The one drawing which would have helped him give it depth was the top view (Fig 11.8). What redeems the carving is probably his long experience with drawing and painting. However, Figure 11.9 shows no trace of squareness as the carver, Eva Linnemann, did not begin by cutting precise profiles but set straight into modelling the forms. The main difference is that Eva has drawn many animals in all sorts of attitudes over the years, so she has a thorough visual memory of them. Her carving may look a little ragged but the life and freedom of the forms are unmistakable.

The deer carved by Howard Spiers, although based on drawings in a book, has been also the subject of much observation. Notice how he has not slavishly followed the outline but kept it rather tubby. Even halfway through one is not reminded of the square block (Figs 11.10–11.16).

FIG 11.10 *Deer in walnut. Note that the shaping is only general.*

FIG 11.11 *Same stage. The front legs are still connected.*

FIG 11.12 *Same stage. Right side.*

FIG 11.13 *Same stage. Rear view.*

FIG 11.14 *The left side is gradually refined.*

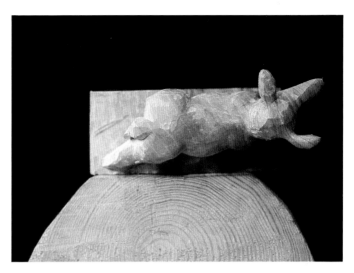

FIG 11.15 *Top view. The squareness of the block has been lost. Even the left side of the animal does not suggest squareness.*

FIG 11.16 *Modelling of the head begun. The wrong positioning of the eyes must be lived with, although they can be made less upward-looking.*

FIG 11.17 *Gradual removal of waste on the right side.*

OTHER DANGERS TO BE AVOIDED

Three dangers remain. One is the cutting out of inside form, between the legs for instance, before the outside shapes have been decided. We have probably all seen legs looking like pieces of string because not enough wood was left on the outside when the spaces between were cut or drilled out. Notice how the piercing between the legs left plenty of waste. They were gradually refined so that they fitted to the body in the right way but also so that they were kept strong until the last (*see* Figs 11.10–11.14, and Figs 11.16–11.23).

The second danger is that the rigidity of the bones is ignored. This can lead to deformities such as 'rubber' legs. The third danger is the itemizing of parts of the anatomy. A careful look at an animal's body, particularly if it is covered with fur or feathers, will show very subtle transitions from rib cage to pelvis to hind leg and from ribcage to shoulder (Fig 11.23), foreleg, neck and jaw. The forms may be quite distinct in places, but not all the way round. The inexperienced have a natural tendency to carve legs and ears as if they were separate and stuck on. Eyes, too, tend to be harshly defined; eyelids are not sharp-edged like the rims of spectacles.

FIG 11.18 *Gradual removal of waste on the left side.*

FIG 11.19 *Rear view with head and body virtually done. Left hind leg almost finished.*

FIG 11.20 *Right side at same stage.*

FIG 11.21 *Right side with legs almost finished.*

FIG 11.22 *Right rear view: carving finished except for left foreleg.*

FIG 11.23 *Base shaped out of the holding block and the surplus removed. Carving finished with Briwax.*

Having learnt the way forms fit together in early pieces you can develop your own style when you know what forms you are simplifying or exaggerating. This is all part of the process of educating your powers of observation. You may have a well-developed sense of design, but without a true knowledge of the forms you are manipulating the design may have no conviction or authority.

THE FINISH

The deer was left showing chisel cuts. Their texture does not pretend to represent fur but does have some of the same light-holding properties.

Howard experimented with various finishes on scrap wood and chose Briwax (Fig 11.23).

THE CARVING'S WEAKNESSES AND STRENGTHS

The photographs show how he gradually worked in towards the form. There are errors, some probably resulting from concentrating on separate anatomical details. The eyes are too close together – at one time they were facing even more dramatically upwards (*see* Fig 11.16) – the legs seem a fraction too short and the head too long. However, despite, or perhaps aided by these failings, the carving has a marvellous vitality.

CHAPTER 12

CARVING THE HUMAN FIGURE

We all think we know the human figure. After all, possession of a human frame would seem to qualify us. However, unless we have made a conscious study of the way it fits together – usually by life drawing or modelling from life or perhaps by anatomical study – we most of us have only a hazy idea. We are taught to name the parts of the body but are not taught how the parts are shaped or fit together. For instance, for most of our purposes the word 'arm' will do. We can identify parts such as shoulder, elbow, upper arm, forearm, wrist, but there is no demand on most of us to know their shapes and how they change when doing different work. Unless we have a superb visual memory we need to make an effort to learn these things (Figs 12.1–12.4).

Whether or not we know the human form well enough, however, many carvers attempt it. This chapter is therefore designed to draw your attention to the things to look out for so that in attempting the project you get more right than wrong.

Of course, a deliberate simplification of the forms is acceptable. A matchstick man will do as a symbol. But most carvings of people seem to be done with a view to capturing the beauty, the power or the movement of the form in a fairly literal way. This means that if observation or memory fails the shapes have to be fudged. To achieve your aims more nearly, knowledge is essential.

LEARNING ABOUT THE HUMAN FORM

The best way to learn is by years of life drawing. If you do not have access to a life class you will at least need an anatomy book and photographs of the nude. Try to use diagrams which look three dimensional – many such books are written with painters most in mind and are not so helpful to the sculptor. Similarly, some photographs are not very informative, looking rather flat.

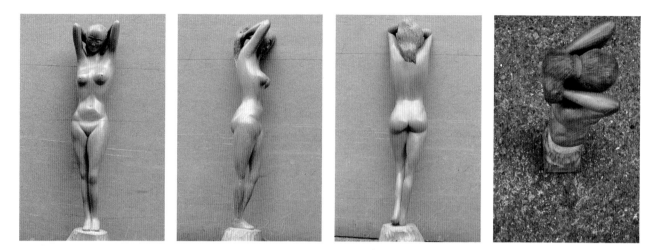

FIGS 12.1–12.4 *Female figure in elm by a student. A charming piece. The carver has a good eye but insufficient knowledge. The area from the waist to the top of the thighs has almost naturalistic voluptuousness but the face is stylized. Armpits are missing and the pubic region is too low in relation to the buttocks. The back is beautiful but a hint of shoulder blades would have enlivened a blank expanse. Lack of planning or cutting too close to the outline has made the lower legs too thin. The top view shows too strong a memory of the squared block it was carved from.*

CHOOSING A FIRST POSE FOR CARVING

It is tempting to carve a figure full of movement or unusual shapes, but you should do this only if you can check by looking in a mirror or at a model how muscles and the relationships of bones change when put under uneven stress. It is best to start with a simple pose which can be given some life by turning the head slightly or varying the positions of the arms.

The example I carved in cherry does not hold a rigid pose. The figure shows how the pelvis tilts and the legs change when the weight is taken on one leg. Experiment by standing in front of a mirror and feeling your own pelvis as you shift weight from one foot to the other (Fig 12.5). If you are plump you will find the forward points of the pelvis (the anterior superior iliac spines) in dimples. If you are lean they may stand out. Notice too how the head of the thighbone (the greater trochanter) sticks out on the leg that takes the weight while the other falls into a hollow. Bone structure determines proportions and gives rigidity (Fig 12.6).

Again, the amount of flesh will affect the appearance. A general rule is that you get an indentation where muscles attach to bone, as muscles are thicker than the tendons that attach them to the bone. Well-developed muscles and fat make these hollows deeper. Such are the two dimples on each side of the spine where it meets the pelvis just above the buttocks (Figs 12.6 and 12.7). These tilt with the pelvis as the legs change position. Muscles in tension contract and tend to bunch and swell. Try pulling with the arm and watch the biceps swell at the top of the upper arm.

VARIATIONS IN PROPORTION

We are all more or less different. A child has proportionally shorter limbs than an adult, and its nose and chin take years to grow to full length.

avoid hitting the thighs when carrying. Our elbows reach just to the top of the pelvis. Our fingertips reach halfway between the hip and the knee. If you turn your palms to face forwards you will find that your hands stand further away from the thighs.

ESSENTIAL POINTS TO REMEMBER

To mention all the points that are of concern to a carver of the human form would fill a book. Apart from those I have already mentioned, I suggest that the main ones are the following. Certainly they are the most commonly forgotten.

THE SPINE, RIBCAGE AND ARMPIT

The spine runs from the pelvis to the skull. Seen from the side it is not straight but follows a gentle S-shape sloping forward to the base of the skull from the top of the ribcage, dropping into the small of the back and out again on the sacrum, the flattened triangle of bone where it joins the pelvis. Between the neck and the small of the back it is slightly curved where it supports the ribcage. The ribcage is almost egg-shaped, with the little end at the top. It slopes forwards from the base of the neck to where the lower ribs divide and the solar plexus is. Its attitude may change but its shape barely does when the body changes position. If you put your hand into your armpit and push a finger up along the ribcage you can feel it sloping in towards the neck. You can also feel the pectoral muscle in front, and behind it the big muscle (latissimus dorsi) that runs from the spine up into the armpit to form the 'pit'. If you raise your arm this muscle can be seen standing out wider than the pectoral muscle, which is the one that the nipple sits on. You can see how when the arm is raised the nipple moves upwards over the ribcage.

FIG 12.5 *Finished male figure. (Note that there is no need to leave gaps between arms and body. There might be small intervals in nature but they would not add anything.)*

Most beginners confuse the hairline with the top of the head and put the eyes too close to the top. In a child the reverse happens, the eyes being about two-thirds of the way down from the crown to the chin. In an adult the centre of the eyes is generally about halfway. A woman has a much wider pelvis than a man. This means that when her feet are together the thighs slope in much more towards the knees. Some men, too, have broad hips. Wide-hipped people have a slight bend in the arm when it is held straight. This is to

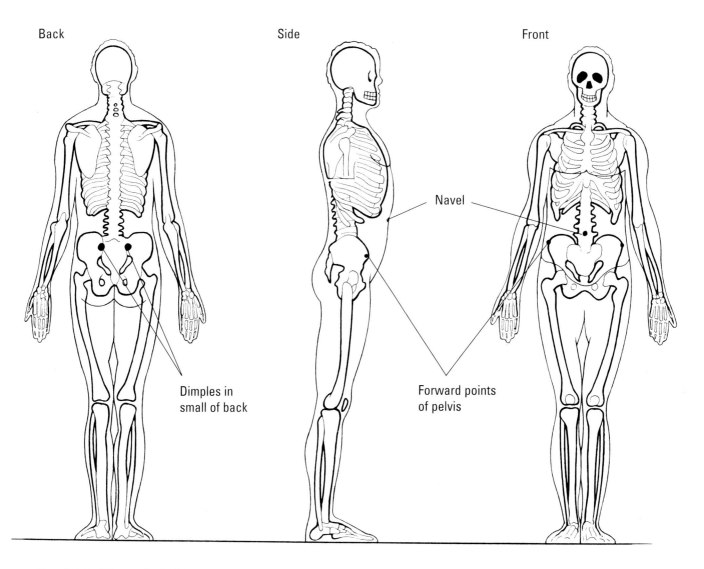

Back

Side

Front

Navel

Dimples in
small of back

Forward points
of pelvis

FIG 12.6 *The male skeleton.*

SHOULDERS

If you can get someone to sit down and let you look straight down on to their shoulders you will see that there is an indentation between the shoulder blades but that from the ridges of these there is a curve forwards to the shoulder (Fig 12.8). When the arm hangs straight down the shoulder blade sticks out (*see* Fig 12.7). The shoulder blade moves forward and around the ribcage at its bottom corner when the arm is raised, and the ridge that runs on to the top of the shoulder (the spine of the scapula) drops beside the spine. There is not a straight line across the back from shoulder to shoulder even on a guardsman. Because of the shoulder blade the top of the arm and the back are continuous. Some carvers are tempted to make the armpit too high or to run a groove between the shoulder and the back as on a doll with movable arms. On the front, however, the head of the upper arm bone (the humerus) and the collarbone (the clavicle) do push the shoulder forward of the ribcage.

HEAD AND NECK

Heads and necks cause many problems. The total height of an adult is about seven and a half times the height of the head. The head tends to be as long from the tip of the nose to the back of the skull as it is tall. Its width outside the ears is about three-quarters of its height. It is essential to remember that the face is only the front part of the head and that most of the head is skull. Seen from above, the skull is oval with a comparatively narrow forehead, the widest part being above and behind the ears (Figs 12.9, 12.10, 12.11). The highest point (the crown) may be here, too. Unless you have a very contrived hairstyle the shape of your skull will shape the hair. The ears, too, push the hair out. I recommend drawing a centre line up the back of the head from the base of the neck, over the top and down through the forehead, nose and chin. The hair may perhaps change in bulk from one side to the other, but symmetry is maintained if it is short even when the head is turned or tilted, so it should be fairly easy to carve the oval of the top view of the head.

CARVING THE FACE

A useful preliminary exercise is to model the skull in clay (Fig 12.12) and then, with the aid of an anatomy book, to build up the muscles (Fig 12.13). When doing the face notice that the temples are usually narrower than the cheekbones (Fig 12.14). These are the widest point of the face on most people, although some have a great width across the back of the jawbones. To get the basic face, carve slopes up from the tip of the nose to the hairline and down from the tip of the nose to the chin. The

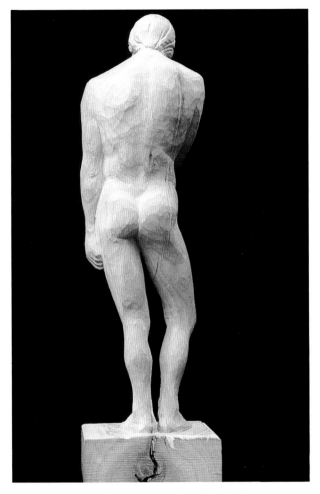

FIG 12.7 *Muscles at the back of the body.*

FIG 12.8 *Top view of carving in progress. Note the hollow between the shoulder blades, the slope forward to the arms and the centre line of neck and head.*

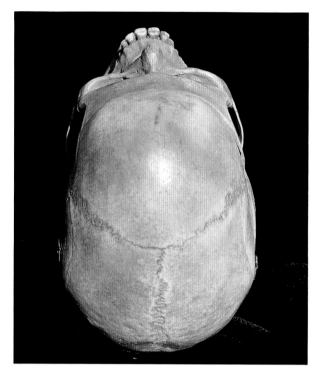

FIG 12.9 *Skull (female) top view.*

FIG 12.10 *A head roughed out in pine without thought of the skull.*

FIG 12.11 *Top view of the same head finished (left) compared with a more accurate head in walnut.*

hairline should be carved in with a deep gouge, not stabbed in. This allows for it to be moved more easily. To continue with the setting-in of the face it is sensible to cut a plane from the side of the nose down to the point of the chin, back to the angle of the jaw and up as far as the cheekbone. Above the cheekbones the temples can be cut in as planes sloping up and back towards the hairline (Fig 12.15).

STARTING THE EYEBALL

A common error when starting the face is to carve grooves under the eyebrows (Fig 12.16). The result is to make the eyes very deep set and corpse-like. The eye is essentially a ball. On most people, too, the brow has a round, fleshy form which overhangs, sometimes obscuring, the top eyelid towards the outside corner. The simplest way to start is to make a deep hollow with a deep gouge (a No. 11 is best) on either side of the nose to create the bridge. This hollow is deep on an adult (Fig 12.17). In order that we may see out of the corner of the eye our eyes are set with the outside corners further back than the inside corners. It is

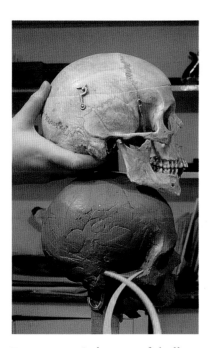

FIG 12.12 *Side view of skull being compared with the early stage of a clay model. The callipers are measuring the length of the zygomatic arch.*

FIG 12.13 *The clay head with most of the muscles.*

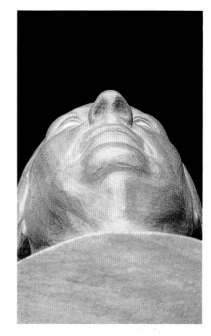

FIG 12.14 *Inka Greene (khaya) by Dick Onians. View under chin. Note how narrow the temple is in relation to the cheeks.*

quite safe to make the hollows on the outside corners too. Although the zygomatic arch (the thin strip of cheekbone at this point) runs back more or less horizontally towards the ear (*see* Fig 12.12), when the face is vertical the effect of flesh and muscles means that you can take a deep gouge and run from the corner of the eye round to the temple, pushing slightly upwards.

THE MOUTH

A mouth is not a straight slot in a spherical head, but is pushed out by a horseshoe of teeth. Top and bottom lips differ. The red part of the lower lip tends to be narrower than the upper and in its middle the part of the lip below the red faces forwards and downwards while the same area at the corner of the mouth slopes sideways and upwards (Fig 12.18).

THE NOSE

Noses are not wedges stuck on the front of a sphere. There is usually a sharp junction around the nostrils, but just below and in front of the eyes the cheek slopes more or less evenly on to the side of the nose.

THE JAW, WINDPIPE AND EAR

Jawbones are not sharp. There is usually a rounded hollow between the neck and the jaw, and the windpipe runs up and forwards towards the chin when seen from the side. The ear, too, is not clearly defined all round but grows out of the back of the jawbone. Ears look complicated and intimidate some carvers, but are in fact beautiful and not too difficult to carve (Fig 12.19). Fortunately for the faint-hearted, hair may be used to conceal them partly or completely.

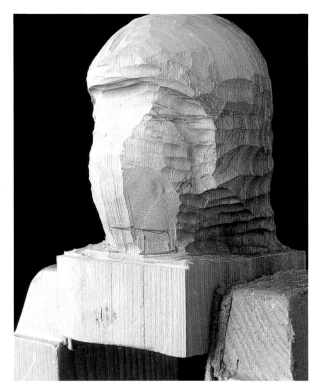

FIG 12.15 *The walnut head roughed out showing the planes of the face prepared after the oval top view had been shaped.*

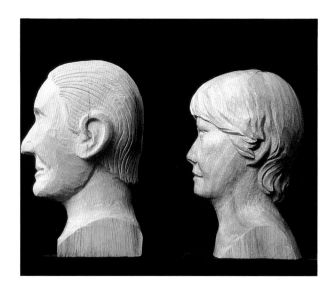

FIG 12.16 *The pine head (left) showing the deeply sunken eyes caused by too deep undercutting of the brows at an early stage. Note also that the mouth is too far back from the tip of the nose, the result of a deep saw cut when roughing out.*

THE NECK

Necks are not cylinders (*see* Figs 12.17, 12.18). There is a muscle that spreads from the base of the skull down towards the shoulders (Fig 12.20). This makes a slope upwards from the collarbones to the back and can cause 'saltcellars' in front. While this trapezius muscle slopes up towards the skull there is a pair of rope-like muscles (the sterno mastoids) that run around the windpipe down from the mastoid process, a lump of bone just behind the ear canal, to the top of the breastbone (the sternum) with small attachments sideways to the collarbones. To see how it is formed look at a thin woman turning her head. The nape of the neck is always higher than the junction of this muscle with the collarbone (*see* Fig 12.17).

BONES AND MUSCLES

Other points to remember are that the arms and legs are neither cylindrical nor made of rubber. The bones give them direction and they bend only at joints. This sense of the rigid underlying form is essential for treatment of the figure. Although muscles and flesh may make limbs appear curved or more or less rounded, they comprise mixtures of hollows, swellings and flattened areas. As with all muscles, it is important that these features are not carved separately. It may be possible to see where a muscle runs from one end to the other but usually they blend subtly with hollows and grooves or ridges, merging with neighbouring flesh in places. The same, of course, is true about any features. Language tends to make us think of ourselves as made up islands of parts, whereas we are covered by a unifying flesh and skin.

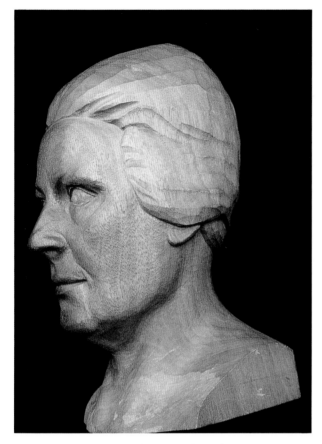

FIG 12.17 *Note the fullness of the brows and the eyeballs and the slope up from cheek to nose. Also visible are the neck muscles.*

FIG 12.18 *The finished walnut head. Note the twisting of the surfaces of the lips.*

THE MIDDLE OF THE BODY

When seen from the side the crutch is higher than the crease under the buttocks. The midpoint of an adult is just above the crutch. The navel is not in the middle of the waist but sits on the upper surface of a ridge of muscle just below it. There is quite a slope down and back from the prominence of the belly to the crutch.

HANDS AND FEET

Hands and feet need careful examination. The palm of the hand is about square and the fingers about the same length as the palm, but the thumb starts from the base of the palm. The foot is not a thin flat plate but is wedge-shaped when seen from the side. The positions of the inner and outer anklebones and the heel need to be watched, particularly their relationship with the bones of the lower leg. The shinbone seems to swing slightly inwards from the knee towards the inner anklebone and the Achilles tendon tapers beautifully down from the calf muscles to the heel on the back. The toes, like the fingers, are not in a straight line at their base. Although the digits may appear curved they are made up of straight bones with flesh and tendons. If they are treated as flat between the knuckles the rubber look should be avoided. When making them distinct, one from another, it is wise

FIG 12.19 *Edward Greene (khaya) by Dick Onians. An older man's head is a sculpture to start with. This was far easier to do than his wife's head. The ears were not hard to do.*

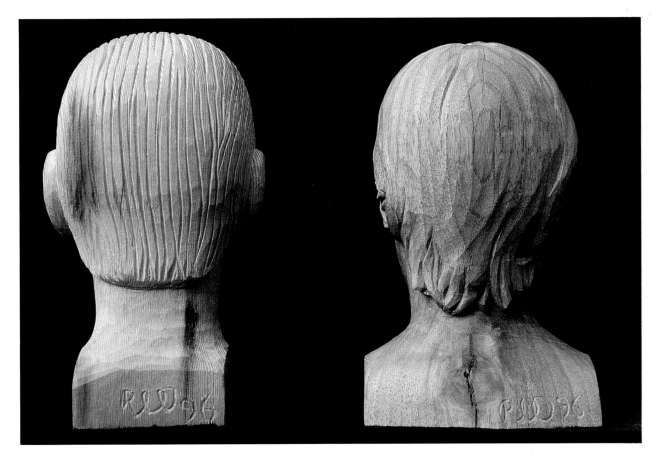

FIG 12.20 *The pine and walnut heads from behind. The neck of the walnut piece is closer to reality.*

not to carve the spaces between them but rather to carve the shape of every digit in turn. This is a general rule which can be applied to the carving of arms against the body and legs when they are close together. The danger lies in making the spaces so wide that the forms around them become too thin. What I have given here are merely guidelines. Observation should come first. The work should be planned with a view to making a figure within your range of knowledge and within what the shape and strength of the wood will allow. If profiles are drawn on the wood they should be cut down to gently, as if the carving were a large, angular balloon which as it shrinks becomes rounded and more detailed. To give sculptural depth always remember the top view and, if anything, exaggerate the way forms recede or project.

CHAPTER 13

STYLIZING THE FIGURE

STYLIZATION IS NOT AN EASY OPTION

The stylized or simplified human or animal sculpture is sometimes used by beginners as a way of making something representational without needing the detailed knowledge of the real form (Fig 13.1). The naïve carver with a good eye uncluttered by exposure to the literal accuracy of sculptures done in the height of the western tradition may capture the strength and impact of the true primitive (Figs 13.2, 13.3), but modern carvers often produce something which fails all round. Proportions may be wrong; limbs may do things not only impossible in nature but also unpleasing in shape or composition. Sometimes parts of the figure may be so close to reality that the whole is a mish-mash of styles.

As I have repeatedly stressed, you need to know how to do something properly before taking liberties with it. There are, of course, people who get trapped in their early academic training and

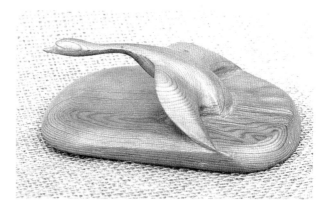

FIG 13.1 *Swan (pine), Dick Onians: an early piece (1962) based on casual observation.*

cannot break out into free expression, but there are far more people who, for want of a sound training of eye and hand, continue producing work of such self-expression that without a written explanation the onlooker is left wondering what it is about. There may be a force or emotional power in such work, but this can simply come from the viewer himself or it may be full of sound and fury, signifying nothing.

FIG 13.2 *Nutcracker (pine), German folk carving: early twentieth century.*

FIG 13.3 *Balinese head. Note the exaggerated line of the brows.*

APPROACHING STYLIZATION

This chapter is not about purely abstract work, where any connection with real objects is imaginary or only hinted at, but about a first stage on the path towards abstraction. When we see any creature we notice certain aspects first: colour, pose, outline, expression. Some or all of these may be contributing to total impact, but in stylization we tend to concentrate on one aspect only. If an image of a jaguar suggests speed we can simplify the animal in such a way that, while we are aware

it is a jaguar we are looking at, we are not distracted by details of fur or claws or exact muscle shape. What we see is everything about the animal that contributes to the idea of speed. We simplify it by eliminating everything that does not emphasize speed and by stressing everything that does.

As I have said elsewhere, the carver (unless aiming for the exact replication which we associate more with model-making) is bound to select and develop forms unconsciously. Stylization is merely making this a conscious process.

VOLUME, MASS AND LINE

There are three main elements in sculpture: volume, mass and line. Volume is inevitable in three-dimensional objects but does not necessarily involve line. A lump of clay or a flint with dents and bumps on it may be amorphous but have an intriguing form. Rounded parts probably look soft, angular parts hard and firm. Something like a sleeping cat may have no sharp outline for the eye to follow but contain plenty of exciting undulations.

Mass is the weight suggested by the object – a seated person's buttocks spread on the seat, or a sleeping cat which sinks into the surface on which it lies, the flesh and fur curving tightly under it (Fig 13.4). In the case of a leaping dancer the mass is directed away from the ground and appears to be reduced or to be concentrated in the direction of movement. To give direction in this case, you need line (Figs 13.5, 13.6).

FIG 13.5. *Line used to express movement.*

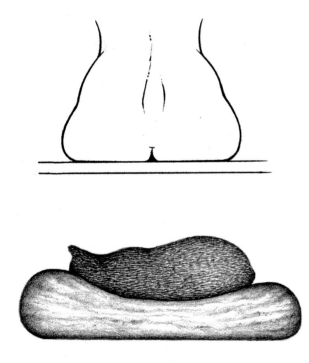

FIG 13.4 *Weight expressed in different ways.*

Line is something the eye travels along. Certain lines suggest certain types of movement (Fig 13.7). Certain shapes enclosed by certain lines suggest particular movement (Fig 13.8).

When you look at any animal or person you can see which of these elements are most involved.

CAPTURING THE ESSENCE

We do not always agree that we see the same thing when we look at a creature. Some will see the strength of the weightlifter pushing up, others will see the weights pushing him down (Fig 13.9).

FIG 13.6 *Odalisque (holly), Dick Onians, showing its linear nature.*

I have found that, if you fix on one impression and hold it while carving, the strength or weight, for example, will come out in the carving. As in a cartoon or caricature there are signposts that one can use. In the case of stylization you are less likely to use facial expression (although this is possible), but posture (body language) should convey the idea by using volume and mass, with or without line. The swelling of muscles, the bending of legs and arms, lengths of limbs, torso and neck can all be exaggerated one way or another to contribute to the effect. Certain lines suggest life, others lifelessness (Fig 13.10).

FIG 13.7 *Lines suggesting types of movement.*

FIG 13.8 *Outlines suggesting particular movement.*

FIG 13.9 *How do you see this – strength pushing up, or weights pushing down?*

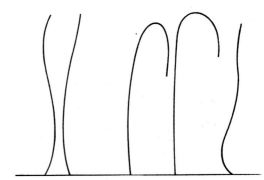

FIG 13.10 *The two lines on the left suggest life. The others suggest lifelessness. They are wilting or collapsing.*

THE COMPOSITION

Once the subject and its main aspect have been chosen, volume, mass and line need to be composed. A carving in the round should read well from all angles unless intended to be seen only from certain positions. Some carvings are meant to be blockish. Generally, however, there should be no suggestion of the rectangular block. To avoid this, the top view must be carefully planned. Twisting the design not only helps with this but also imparts life. To make a good composition forms and lines can be made to balance one another, echoing or reflecting, flowing together as the viewpoint is changed or forming deliberate contrasts.

AN ILLUSTRATION OF STYLIZATION

The subject is a carving of a mother swinging her baby around. This is developed from an old representational carving of mine (Fig 13.11).

The task was to convey the movement by simplifying and developing forms. Apart from the composition and the movement there is also the love between mother and child, which, like the movement, has to be felt while you are carving if it is to come through in the finished piece.

PREPARATORY SKETCHES

Simple lines may be drawn to suggest the movement, but apart from the difficulty of carving thin forms with short grain there is no suggestion of there being two people or of any emotion between them. The first difficulty is overcome by making less spindly forms, the second by including symbolic heads in appropriate attitudes (Fig 13.12).

MAKING A MAQUETTE

After making some sketches to arrive at the composition it is helpful to make a maquette

FIG 13.11 *Mother swinging baby (lime), Dick Onians.*

(model). If you use clay or Plasticine you need a frame or armature of stiff material (Fig 13.13). I recommend square-section aluminium armature wire which is available in various thicknesses. I used 3mm (⅛in) wire. Thinner wire can be fastened to it to help support thin forms or be wound round the thicker wire to stop the modelling material from collapsing. Here I drilled a 3mm (⅛in) hole in a slab of wood and rammed the armature wire into it for strong anchorage.

Maquettes are very useful but can be dangerous to the final carving. Clay and wood are essentially different. If a clay model is

FIG 13.12 *Essays in stylization.*

followed too closely the woodcarving may end up looking like clay. Furthermore, carving involves the carver's response to the wood and to shapes that arise as he works in towards the final piece. Some shapes may be more promising than those he made in the maquette. A maquette should help to organize the shape so that it works well in three dimensions, and in this case it also means getting a good top view. It helps

with roughing out the wood and gives opportunities to work out details that would be difficult to express in a drawing (Fig 13.14).

CHOICE OF WOOD

For this piece I needed a wood that was particularly strong as the arms and the child's body are long with some weight being taken on thin sections. The design was laid on the wood with the

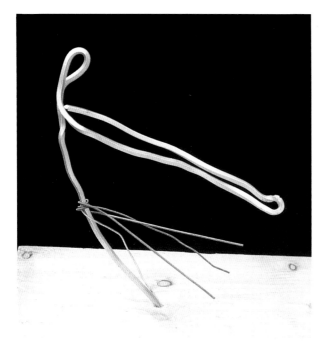

FIG 13.13 *Aluminium and steel wire armature for stylized version of mother swinging baby.*

FIG 13.14 *Clay maquette showing the modelling tools used.*

grain running along the arms. The body is thin in the maquette and is short-grained from the waist to the breast, but in the wood could be left thicker. If it showed any sign of breaking I could break it cleanly and dowel it for strength. Such joins are virtually invisible if done carefully – but this is a difficulty best avoided. Ash was chosen because it was available as well as strong. It is not a wood I recommend for carving as it is tough when seasoned; it yields to strong blows and tends to be stringy, not cutting crisply. This piece was slow grown and therefore comparatively easy.

ROUGHING OUT – THE USE OF MACHINERY

The outline was roughed out first with a chain saw (Fig 13.15). This is dangerous to the user and can also cut off too much from the object. I followed this with a rotary cutter on an angle grinder. Like the chain saw, this is difficult to control and is obviously limited as to what cuts

can be made. The resulting shape is therefore rough and far too big. This method is probably conducive to more sculptural carving than a bandsaw, which tends to create profiles at right angles to each other and which is often taken too close to the finished outline.

There can be no reasonable objection to the use of machinery in the roughing out stage provided that the result is what you intended. Purists who object to their use might as well insist on all trees being felled and squared with axe and adze.

Always keep the offcuts – you never know what may go wrong (*see* Fig 13.15). Shakes may be filled and dead knots in the middle of the wood and pieces carved away in error be more easily replaced with a piece of matching grain if a wide variety of offcuts is kept.

If you have no machinery the same stage must be reached with axe, saw or gouge, which can be satisfying to do but takes longer. You are certainly less likely to take too much away.

WORKING INTO THE FORM

It is interesting to note that at the roughing-out stage you may have a good sculpture which conveys most of what you wish (Fig 13.16). Notice how the forms are shaped by working around them with a deep gouge, occasionally running along a form to develop the line (Fig 13.17). Little undercutting is allowed at first, partly to keep options open to change the sculpture and partly for strength (Fig 13.18). If you carve around the forms hollows between them gradually appear. The space between the body and the arms gains a hole only after the shapes of the body and the arms are well defined. Notice how a column is left between the rim of the mother's skirt and the child's arms, at first so that pressure can be applied to the child's body and skirt; later so that shock waves caused by vigorous mallet work on the

rest of the sculpture do not travel along the arms and shatter them (Fig 13.19).

ANCILLARY TOOLS AND FINISHING

As the shapes are mostly long curves it is helpful to use rifflers, rasps or Surforms. On a softer wood they may be dispensed with but they can reduce the amount of banging with a mallet, particularly on end grain of hard woods. I still recommend the use of chisels to pare down to the final surface. In this case, where possible, cuts follow the flow of the design. This teaches good chisel control, emphasizes the forms and shows the colour and grain of the wood more crisply and with less effort than sandpaper.

There is no rule that dictates or bans the use of any tool or any finish on completely original work such as this. Taste may reject a smooth and shiny surface as making the wood resemble plastic. On the other hand, rough texturing

FIG 13.15 *Block chain sawn, with main offcuts.*

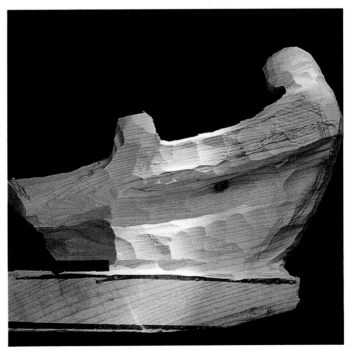

FIG 13.16 *The main outline is already there after roughing out with the angle grinder. Note the dark dead knot below the arms.*

could reduce the richness of the grain, make the work look folksy or, if not done carefully, make it look unfinished.

Something which has long, slender forms like this needs a clean line, so sandpapering this could make sense. A compromise I suggest, although I have not used abrasive paper here, is to get as smooth a chiselled finish as possible and then wipe it lightly with flour (00 grade) paper. This will reduce unwanted facets and remove nibs without dulling the figure of the wood.

Because even Danish oil darkens the wood and I like the natural colour of ash, I have protected the surfaces of this piece with Renaissance Wax (Fig 13.20).

THE BASE

Finally, the base is reduced in size, or it could be removed altogether and a smarter, contrasting material be used instead.

For exhibition purposes I should prefer to screw it on to an oval base of grey or green slate or dark marble. The weight of the stone will give stability. When shaping this wooden base I had to make sure not only that it would complement the piece but also that the sculpture would not tip over. If the carving is going into a gallery or anywhere else where it might be knocked the base should also extend a little further out than the sculpture all around. In this case an oval base would protect it and complement it as several lines in the sculpture have long curves and the two skirts are essentially oval.

The moment you venture into consciously interpretative or stylized work you are making your own rules and so choices of shape, texture and finish are entirely yours. My comments are not prescriptive but simply the result of making and looking at carvings for many years (Figs 13.21, 13.22).

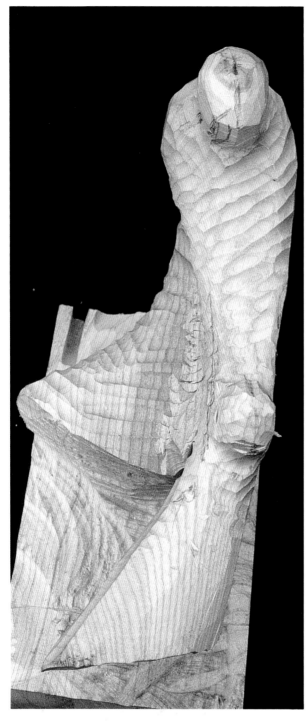

FIG 13.17 *Top view after first shaping with gouge. Note the cuts going across the form. No penetration between the arms yet. The broad, flat treatment of the child's dress emphasizes the line.*

FIG 13.18 *Right side showing development of the forms, with the chisels used at this stage.*

FIG 13.19 *The child's arms and the mother's skirt are kept attached by a pillar that gradually diminishes.*

FIG 13.20 *Left side of finished piece showing the base.*

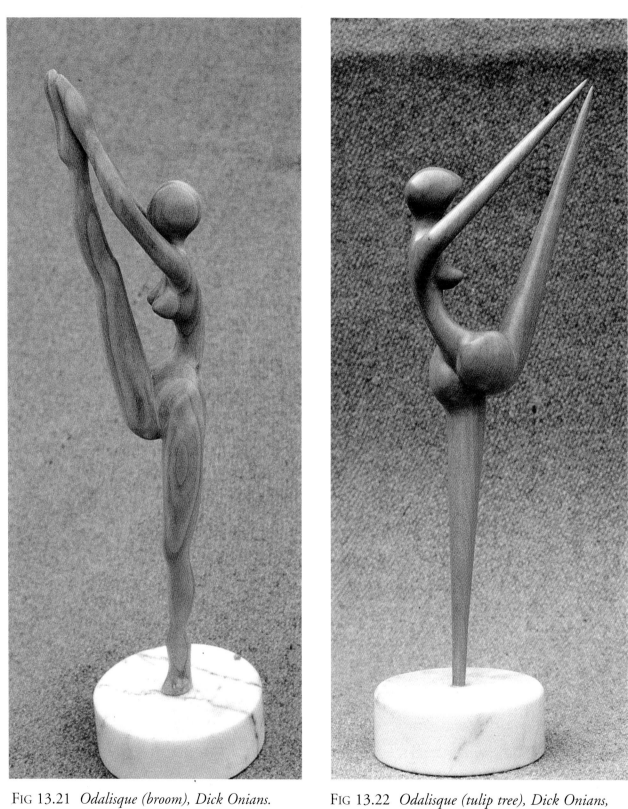

FIG 13.21 *Odalisque (broom), Dick Onians.*

FIG 13.22 *Odalisque (tulip tree), Dick Onians, showing a further degree of stylization.*

CHAPTER 14

CARVING AN ABSTRACT

At an exhibition of my abstract carvings someone once recommended that I make birds, things that people like him could understand. I wonder how many people do understand birds. Picasso, asked what an abstract of his meant, is alleged to have plucked a rose and asked his interrogator what it meant. What both doubters must have had in mind was that they liked things that they could recognize from the real world, items that had conventionally been represented by artists and craftsmen, and, incidentally, things which by their closeness to nature showed man's mastery of the material and tools.

Yet people who profess not to like abstract art often enjoy unusual shapes in nature such as are found in decayed parts of trees, in stones or clouds; they may also enjoy the shapes of cars, of elements of ornament on buildings and furniture, or the shapes of geometrical solids. If they insist that they like these things because they are practical then one might wonder what practical value there is in a landscape painting or a portrait.

Artists shed new light on the world around us. We all have an individual way of looking at the world. We may express this in an art form. The vision may be banal or inadequately expressed, but often it reveals a truth we had not suspected, shows a familiar theme in a new light, excites or disturbs us in nameless ways or presents a completely new idea which fills us with wonder or delight.

If one asks why anyone should want to make abstract shapes, one might as well speculate why anyone should choose to make representational objects, except as by a sort of cultural momentum. Moreover, since the arrival of the camera and modern casting techniques, copying what is done so much better by nature is no longer so important.

Unless the artist needs to sell and knows that no one will buy his abstracts, there is no reason for not producing them. True artists, however, are the people who make things because they need to make them, not because they need to sell them. Some may starve in garrets.

Making abstract art because you cannot make representational pieces is feasible. By copying from nature and from traditional styles, however, the carver builds an understanding of forms and how things fit together. Abstract art attempted afterwards is more likely to succeed. Some art schools now discourage students from copying old examples and even from working directly from nature. It is felt that it somehow prevents the artist from directly and honestly expressing inner thoughts and feelings: that ineradicable habits of technique and thought can be developed which are derived from other people. My own experience as both teacher and artist is that, after mastering technique and developing vision, a good artist will make his own style and, if he wishes to communicate, he will use a 'language' to which viewers can respond. People who are merely talented (as opposed to artists) may, it is true, become set in ways which limit honest and free expression. The free-for-all approach, however, may thwart their natural talent and produce what may, while very therapeutic for the creator, be unintelligible to the onlooker. While it is very easy to make an abstract piece, it is very difficult to make a good one.

In abstract work most people make the things they would like to see. Some follow an instinct and let the shapes emerge, presumably led by their subconscious (Fig 14.1). In such work artists are, of course, making their own rules and, provided they are happy with the result, we need say no more. If artists wish others to respond positively, however, (it is not necessary for people to like a piece of art for it to be good) they should consider the principles of three-dimensional design.

Some sculptors believe that a piece should have one main viewpoint. This is obviously the case with pieces attached to walls or in niches. Others, like Rodin, believe that work should read well all around. If you can see very distinct front, back and sides this

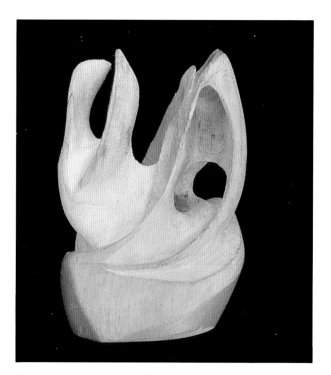

FIG 14.1 *A student's first carving (jelutong). He followed his instinct and worked on it over several years, but still could not make all the forms pull together.*

must be intentional. Such a piece, although appearing static, can be very impressive, like an obelisk. If a sculpture has incongruous elements, for instance if the front is covered with fine detail and the back consists of large blunt shapes, the contrast has to be deliberate and relevant. If one side consists of angular projections and the reverse of rounded forms, the transition has to appear intended. Fairy stories are patently untrue, yet if they did not contain a deeper truth, or were inconsistent with their own code, no one would bother with them. If you make your own rules they should be consistent and have their own logic.

Apart from the wholeness of the sculpture, other aspects to consider are balance, line and rhythm. Sculptural depth is essential. This means that the shapes must be strong and neither lost in minute detail nor ill defined.

THE INSPIRATION

AN INTERESTING PIECE OF WOOD

The starting-point needs thought. Some carvers take a piece of wood, usually of an interesting or at least asymmetrical shape, and without a plan start delving with the chisel. If the wood is sufficiently knobbly or sinuous little may need to be done to draw attention to the rhythms and apparent forces in the original piece (Fig 14.2). A weathered rootstock or stem covered with growths can be very inspiring. The problem that can arise is that, while the thing has balance and suggests the same movements when viewed from most directions, it may have elements that cannot be reconciled with

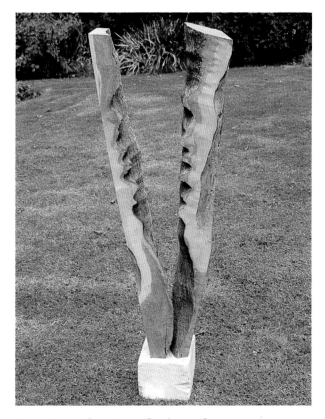

FIG 14.2 *This piece of oak was being cut into a fence post when it fell apart to reveal this strange double ripple. The forester gave it to me. I merely planed the square sides and arranged it on a plinth. To do more would spoil it.*

what seems to be emerging. Sometimes a part of the piece which has been laboured over for hours has to be cut away. These hours will have not been wasted; all the time devoted to carving has been practice for the carver's artistic judgement. But it can be very frustrating and is not helpful if you hope to make a living by it. Before beginning on such a piece of wood it is wise to reflect whether anything you can do will improve on nature. It may be better to preserve it as it is but study it, draw it, even, as Henry Moore used to do, make a plaster cast from it and then add to or subtract from the cast, until a satisfactory shape has been achieved. Then any copy in wood, or another material that may be more appropriate, will have a unity and your own stamp.

NATURAL PHENOMENA

This approach applies when taking inspiration from a natural object which has definite form: the flow of water, the power of a toadstool thrusting the earth aside as it swells up from under the ground, the pressure of a hard object against a soft one. The natural form should be observed closely with drawings and, possibly, models until you are in a position to 'abstract' the essence of it in such a simplified form that it is only the principle that is demonstrated and not the original shape (Figs 14.3–14.5).

MICROSCOPY AND MATHEMATICS

Microscopy has revealed unusual shapes and patterns which are new and exciting for us. These are very stimulating and may be used. Geometrical forms such as cones, pyramids and spheres may be arranged in multiples (Fig 14.6) or combined in groups of various shapes or sizes to make pleasing or even powerful patterns (Fig 14.7). There are also notions such as the 'Möbius' band or unending surface and other apparently impossible mathematical puzzles (Figs 14.8, 14.9).

FIG 14.3 *Moving water.*

FIG 14.4 *Drawings developing the shapes in moving water.*

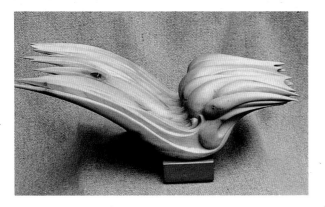

FIG 14.5 *'Ripple' – tulip tree carving derived from the bottom drawing (Dick Onians).*

THREE-DIMENSIONAL DOODLES

If you take a piece of ribbon or a rubber band or soft aluminium armature wire you can make some very pleasing shapes. To copy these in wood is a useful exercise, and the wood will make them into beautiful objects. But these shapes could easily be made with steel or plastic strip. When using wood you should exploit its unique properties. Because wood is carved out of the solid, sides do not need to be parallel or even. Thicknesses can be varied. Ripples, swellings, angular extrusions can be included. For instance, if you bend a bar in an arc its surface area does not change. By adding bulk on

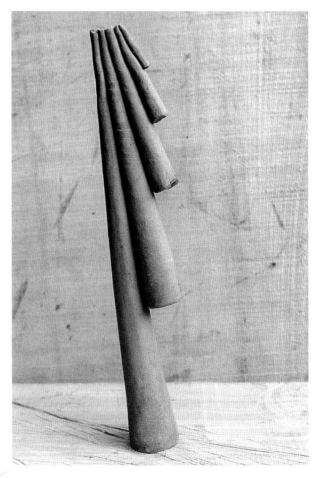

FIG 14.6 *Experimental Plasticine model showing combinations of a simple form.*

FIG 14.7 *'Vortex' – carving in elder employing the same idea as in the Plasticine model (Dick Onians).*

FIG 14.8 *'Discontinuity' – carving in tulip tree wood attempting the impossibility of making a dotted line in 3D (Dick Onians).*

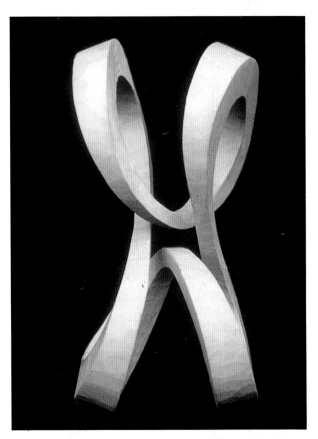

FIG 14.9 *'Möbius 8' – lime (Dick Onians). If you run your finger along the surface you pass over the whole sculpture and find yourself back where you started.*

FIG 14.10 *A sculpture on the theme of 'Compression' in cedar of Lebanon by Zena Michael.*

the tightest part of the curve movement is suggested. The reverse can show pressure (Fig 14.10). Tension can be implied by taking a straight bar and making it thin in the middle (Fig 14.11).

HARDNESS AND SOFTNESS

Observing how materials behave and developing their natural tendencies can produce powerful results. If two arms are pressed together the flesh squeezes out where they touch. These curvatures suggest pressure, and you could make a sculpture which develops this effect (Fig 14.12). As rounded forms look soft, perhaps floppy, the contrast provided by hard, angular forms can redeem a potential blob by suggesting strength or movement and at the same time emphasize the point about squeezed objects.

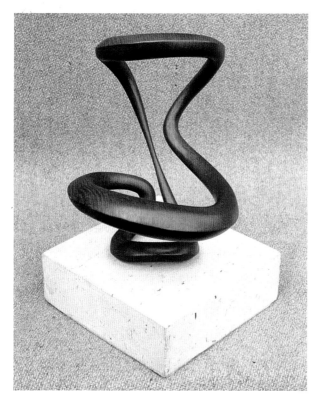

FIG 14.11 *'In Torque' – a mahogany carving with a line drawn thin in the middle for the sake of tension (Dick Onians).*

FIG 14.12 *'Zeugma' – a pine carving showing two soft forms pressed together (Dick Onians).*

EXPLOITING THE PROPERTIES OF WOODCARVING

Admittedly, clay or plaster built on an armature can produce the same shapes as those mentioned above. However, wood produces its own effect, partly because the material has a different psychological and physical appeal and partly because the process of working with wood allows you to deviate from (and improve on) the original plan in ways which other materials would not suggest (Figs 14.13, 14.14).

People who work with wood do it with love. This is often quite enough to give the sculpture a special impact. Furthermore, if while working the carver really feels the magic, the tenderness, the power, or whatever other sensation the shape is meant to convey, it will probably affect viewers in the same way.

The least that can be said about an abstract work of art is that it is itself; but then, the same could be said of a rose.

FIG 14.13 *Wire maquette with Plasticine sphere inserted.*

FIG 14.14 *'Möbius Sling' – catalpa carving based on the wire and Plasticine maquette (Dick Onians).*

CHAPTER 15

INCISED LETTERING

LETTERING IS PART OF THE MESSAGE

'If BRIX don't spell bricks what do it spell then?' is an old joke and unanswerable. It is surely enough that the message is intelligible; the way in which it is expressed is unimportant. There is many a message incorrectly or awkwardly expressed that we see and understand. We may think less of the writer if there are gross errors of spelling, grammar or fact, but we seldom notice letter forms and their spacing unless they are unreadable. Unconsciously we are disturbed by flawed letter forms and poor spacing. An inscription well formed is a joy to look at close up and from afar.

Lettering is more than just the words of the message. The arrangement of shapes on paper or tablet is as much an art form in lettering as in drawing or relief sculpture. Slovenly or uneducated lettering may indicate a contempt for the message or for the reader. It is certain that well-ordered lettering is clear and attractive. It may lend dignity or poetry to the words and, indeed, is part of the message.

LAZY AND SERIOUS APPROACHES TO LETTERING

When drawing up an inscription an easy way out is to use transfer letters. This may take care of the letter shapes but the layout and spacing are still yours. When it comes to letter cutting, a pantograph with a router may be used. However, the result is boring precision and regularity. To produce the liveliness, subtlety and freedom that is seen in the best inscriptions you need to study the letter forms and practise cutting freehand.

LEARNING FROM A GOOD MODEL

The most important alphabet used in western culture is that of the Roman capitals. The generally accepted best model is the inscription on the base of Trajan's Column, a plaster cast of which is in the Victoria and Albert Museum in London (Fig 15.1). The Roman alphabet did not have J, U and W, and the Trajan's Column inscription also lacks H, K, Y and Z. These last four have been borrowed from other inscriptions. They and the other three letters have been developed to match the style. Over the centuries the shapes of the letters have been modified by custom and by individuals. From this you can see that when you are experienced you may develop your own style by varying proportions, thicknesses and letter forms to suit your own taste or the demands of the space available.

TOOLS FOR PRACTICE

Before you can take such liberties you need to know what you are taking liberties with. It is generally believed that the carved letter forms originated with brush or pen strokes and were probably painted on the stone before being cut. To practise the forms, therefore, you will need an A2 or A3 layout pad and a flat-ended lettering brush 6mm (¼in) wide such as a Daler Dalon 88. A piece of balsa wood 6mm (¼in) wide with a thin edge or the same width of veneer set in the end of a pencil-sized dowel may serve as a pen, or you may use any broad, flat-ended pen. Gouache or ink will suffice for the brush and the balsa pen. You may also practise using two pencils fastened together.

First, you need to copy the letters from a good model with a single pencil line. I suggest you use a sharp, softish pencil (B or 2B), a ruler and a set square. By drawing the shape of each letter of the alphabet at least twice about 35mm (1½in) high you should fix the shapes in your mind. The examples drawn here (Fig 15.2) have some of the

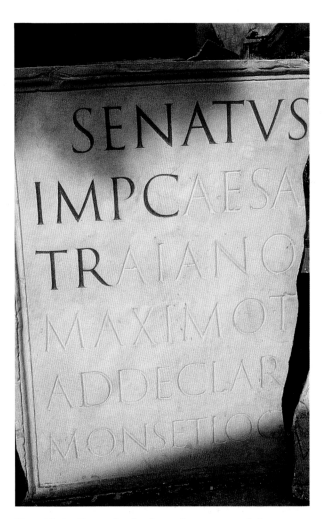

FIG 15.1 *Part of a broken plaster cast of the inscription on Trajan's column. Part of the inscription has been painted in, as the original would have been. Notice that the lower letters are smaller. The inscription was originally meant to be seen from below and so the letters would all have seemed the same size. The Ss are composed of two circles, the top one being slightly smaller than the lower. This means that the width of the letter is about half its height. B, E, F, K, L, P, R and J follow the same proportions. The C, D, G, O and Q fit in a square and their outer lines contain, visually, the same area. The A, H, N, T, U, X, Y and Z fit in a rectangle which visually has the same area as the O. Their counters, not being enclosed, are more easily judged by half-closed eyes.*

FIG 15.2 *The Roman alphabet, originally drawn by Philip Surey.*

idiosyncrasies of Philip Surey who drew it originally, but it serves well. The chunky shapes are suited to cutting in wood. He carves letters by short, stabbing strokes or by chasing. These methods give a curve to the whole length of the side of a straight member. This means that his serifs are not as tapered as I cut them.

SPACING

You will notice from your own efforts that some of the letters look crowded and others too separate. When you design inscriptions you will see that the spacing is as important as the letter shapes. L followed by T could leave a vast space between them but they do not become entangled easily, whereas C or F followed by T could. If you get them as close as possible without crowding them you will need to get a similar space between other letters. This space is something which cannot be measured mathematically but has to be judged by eye.

INDIVIDUAL LETTERS

Next, you need to practise the individual letters using the thick and thin strokes. First, draw parallel lines at about 35mm (1½in) intervals with about one-third of the letter height (11mm, ½in) between each pair of lines. At the beginning of each line carefully draw the letter that you are going to practise. Load your brush with gouache or your pen with ink or gouache and fill in the pencil letter with careful strokes (Fig 15.3). The end of the pen or brush (Fig 15.4) is held at 30° to the top line and drawn straight down to form a broad vertical stroke. By tilting it slightly one way or the other a thicker or a thinner line is formed. Trial runs with the drawing implement on scrap paper give confidence.

FIG 15.3 *A left foot serif being edged out freehand with a balsa pen. Note the angle of 30° drawn above the left-hand example to illustrate the tilt of the pen. There are ten strokes of the pen held at 30° to show the relationship between pen width and height of letter.*

FIG 15.4 *Ending the bottom lobe of B on a practice sheet using a flat-ended brush with gouache. Note the criticism of the As on the upper line. This is good practice.*

CHARACTERISTIC ASPECTS OF ROMAN CAPITALS

Although you can see their shapes clearly drawn here, it is worth pointing out certain characteristics of the Trajan capitals and the names of the parts of letters (Figs 15.5 and 15.6). Other points not covered by the photographs and drawings are given below.

The C and G are based on the D but flatten

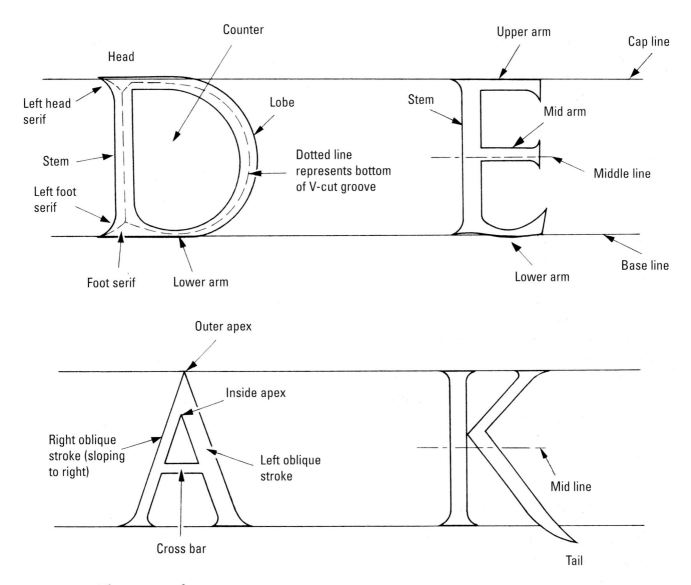

FIG 15.5 *The naming of parts.*

out towards the serifs. It is very difficult to get this effect without making the letters square. The serifs on the ends of curves should be kept small.

The tails of R and K can be treated variously. If they terminate on the line in a serif they can look very heavy. If they curl up and rest just on the line they can look inadequately supported and also make a large gap if followed by a letter which slopes away, like A or M. When you have experience you may join this tail with the serif of

the following letter or even boldly cross its stroke. A good solution is to drop the tail of the R or K below the line, thus being able to reduce the gap between the letters. With these letters it is essential that they look as if they are neither falling over backwards nor kicking the following letter.

The tail of J is best taken below the line. You may end it with a serif or let it taper gracefully.

W and U are difficult, as the Romans did not use them. U appeared as a capital in the Middle

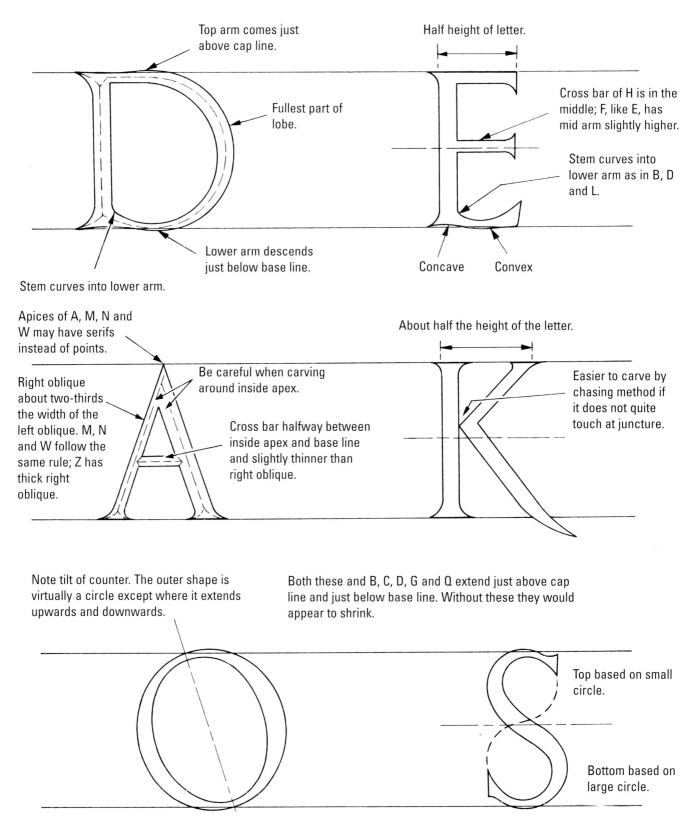

Top arm comes just above cap line.

Fullest part of lobe.

Lower arm descends just below base line.

Stem curves into lower arm.

Half height of letter.

Cross bar of H is in the middle; F, like E, has mid arm slightly higher.

Stem curves into lower arm as in B, D and L.

Concave   Convex

Apices of A, M, N and W may have serifs instead of points.

Be careful when carving around inside apex.

Right oblique about two-thirds the width of the left oblique. M, N and W follow the same rule; Z has thick right oblique.

Cross bar halfway between inside apex and base line and slightly thinner than right oblique.

About half the height of the letter.

Easier to carve by chasing method if it does not quite touch at juncture.

Note tilt of counter. The outer shape is virtually a circle except where it extends upwards and downwards.

Both these and B, C, D, G and Q extend just above cap line and just below base line. Without these they would appear to shrink.

Top based on small circle.

Bottom based on large circle.

FIG 15.6 *Characteristic features of the lettering on Trajan's column.*

Ages, and V was used until then. The French still call W *double V*. Sometimes two Vs are interlocked. The crossover has to be nicely judged so that the serifs do not become overcrowded. In his drawing Philip Surey has managed to avoid this without making the letter look too wide. Sometimes the letter is formed in the same way but without extending the crossed arms to the top line. This means that the outside of the apex is below the top line. If the apex is taken to the top line the letter may look too wide. You should not make it like an upside down M as the angles are quite different. The middle V shape of the M has an angle of about 52°, but the angle with the outer strokes is more acute. On the original inscription on Trajan's column the outer left oblique strokes start at a flatter angle, but modern letterers usually make M symmetrical. With M the important things to look for are the regular spacing of the bases of the strokes. The internal distance between the outside oblique strokes and the point is the same on each side. Care must be taken to keep the letter from doing the splits or looking as though it is falling apart at the centre.

The tops of R and P are similar but not the same. The top of the R is both wider and deeper. The bottom of the counter is enclosed. The stroke diminishes to the bottom right of the lobe then returns horizontally, keeping the arm the same thinness, to end in the vertical stroke. The P, on the other hand, is not quite closed. The tail of the lobe curves up to but does not quite meet the stem.

The same gap can be made in the U if the stem on the right has a foot serif (usually on the outside of the right stem only). In Philip Surey's example (*see* Fig 15.2) the left-hand stem has the full thickness, but it diminishes as it curves across the base then runs up in a thin right stem. Others carry the curve around, diminishing it to its lowest part in the middle and then swelling it

slightly as it rises to touch the right stem above the serif.

S is probably the most difficult letter to draw and carve because the serifs are easily made too heavy. Care is also needed to prevent its appearing to topple over. It is based on two circles that just kiss, the bottom one being slightly larger than that at the top.

The mid-point of Y is just below its inside angle.

The Trajan inscription shows a slight curvature to the lower strokes of V, M and W before they come to a point. This entasis also occurs on the bottom of the oblique stroke of N. It stops the points looking too sharp.

TRANSFERRING A LETTERING DESIGN ON TO WOOD

Several attempts are needed before you will be satisfied with the design, spacing and letter shapes. This must be done on paper unless you are very experienced. Pencil used straight on wood dents the surface and is difficult to correct. Once the design is complete it is transferred to the wood with carbon paper, though this has the disadvantage that it is not easy to rub out. If you transfer the parallel lines with carbon paper, minimum pressure is required to prevent denting of the wood where it will not be cut away (Fig 15.7).

TECHNIQUES OF CUTTING LETTERS IN WOOD

CHOICE OF WOOD

The ideal wood for lettering is dense, fine textured and close grained. A light-coloured wood shows the shadows well, although painted letters look good in dark wood. Beech, cherry, pear and sycamore are excellent. The context may demand

FIG 15.7 *Alphabet drawn by Janet Monks being transferred to an oak board with the aid of carbon paper.*

a less suitable wood. Oak is often used successfully but care is needed to prevent its crumbling in the sharp angles, particularly the inside apices of A, K, M, N, W, V, X and Y. Durable woods such as teak and iroko are most appropriate for exposure to weather, but are crumbly like oak and likely to have interlocked grain. Lime is too soft to take letters crisply. The most stable panels are of quarter-sawn wood (*see* Chapter 2).

The troughs of the letters are designed to catch the light, so the angle of the sides depends partly on where the lettering is to be seen. The angle of the V-shaped troughs of the Trajan's Column inscription is 110° but that was in stone, painted and in a land of bright sunlight. On plain wood an angle of 90° makes for legibility. An angle of 60° is suitable for a highly figured wood but is difficult to carve by the chasing method. As the angle is the same for thick and for thin strokes the thin strokes are shallower than the thick, and where they meet look like hanging valleys. A useful prop is a template of card with the appropriate angle which can check the grooves. If it is marked with the different depths of stems, right and left oblique strokes and horizontals, it will be useful in maintaining consistent depths.

TWO BASIC TECHNIQUES

There are two basic techniques used in letter cutting: stabbing and chasing. Chasing means pushing the chisel along the shape of the letter. Some letterers use a series of short stabs for both the middle of a stroke and for the sides; others only stab centre lines and chase the rest. This is slow but produces subtle shapes. It is the only way to carve very big letters. To stab all the parts of letters requires a vast range of tools, particularly gouges of various sweeps and widths, some with rounded-over ends and some straight across, so a compromise is needed. Cutting with a V tool is not recommended; it is very difficult, as one side of the chisel inevitably goes against the grain on curves and diagonals.

THE DIRECTION OF THE GRAIN

Most lettering in wood is done with the line of script running along the grain. As most straight strokes are perpendicular to the cap and base lines, cutting is across the grain. It is far safer and quicker than stabbing along the grain as any vagaries such as spiral, wavy or interlocked grain cause least trouble. If a cut along the grain is stabbed in from the side the wood fibres may be torn. Cuts along the grain are best done by stabbing in the ends of serifs to prevent splitting, stabbing the centre line and finally chasing the sides of the cut, taking care to push the chisel in the direction least likely to catch in the grain. This can be a problem if you work on a board fixed to a wall. Ambidexterity is a great help when lettering on fixed vertical panels.

THE STABBING METHOD

The method of letter cutting described here involves stabbing at least the central line and, where possible, the whole shape except the serifs. This is the quickest way. The shapes of the serifs, however, can look too heavy unless care is taken.

Straight Strokes

If you stab the straight strokes it is sensible to acquire straight-edged chisels which are wide enough to fit between the inner slopes of the serifs. It is hard to stab long strokes with several cuts of a narrow chisel without the lines wandering. For letters 38mm (1½in) high you need a straight-edged chisel 32mm (1¼in) wide. This leaves 3mm (⅛in) at top and bottom for the serifs. A carpentry chisel can be used, but you get better cuts from one bevelled on both sides. You also need others to fit the shorter straight strokes (Figs 15.8, 15.9).

Curved Letters

If you have gouges of many sweeps and sizes you can stab most of the curved letters but you will need to chase sometimes. If you do not have a gouge or

FIG 15.8 *Stabbing the centre line of a straight letter with a No. 1 chisel which reaches from the inside point of the serif to level with the inner point of the V.*

FIG 15.9 *The first cut sloping in at 45° from the inside edge. By starting from this side the pressure is taken off the point of the V.*

FIG 15.10 *A gouge with a matching shape being used to stab the centre line of an O.*

FIG 15.11 *A skew chisel with about 70° angle at its tip being used to chase the outside curve of the counter of an O.*

FIG 15.12 *A round-ended No. 3 gouge being used to stab in the inward-facing curve of an O.*

FIG 15.13 *A large gouge stabbing in the inward-facing curve of an O.*

FIG 15.14 *A round-ended No. 3 gouge stabbing in the outward facing curve of the counter of an O.*

gouges which more or less fit vertically on the centre lines of curved parts of letters you have to stab the centres with several cuts from narrow gouges about 6mm (¼in) wide. As far as possible the sweep should match the curve (Fig 15.10), but a shallow gouge such as a No. 4 or 5 (English), No. 3 or 5 (Swiss), will do. The sloping sides of the letters are then chased out with a skew chisel about 12mm (½in) wide with an angle of about 70° at the point (Fig 15.11), or with a nearly flat gouge (No. 3 English or No. 2 Swiss) of similar width with its end slightly rounded. Care has to be taken when chasing that the thickness of the side of the tool does not foul the opposite slope nor the edge dig deeper in the centre than desired. The sides of the tool may need to be ground thin so that the metal does not squeeze against the sides of the cut. On inward-facing curves the skew chisel digs in or 'chatters'. The bull-nosed nearly flat gouge works well either chasing or stabbing (Fig 15.12). If you do have appropriately shaped gouges you will find that a slightly flatter or larger gouge than the one that stabbed the centre line can stab in the sloping sides of inside curves. It will pick up the outside line as it goes in (Fig 15.13). All that is needed then is for it to be rocked to each side to meet the bottom of the trough. The outward-facing curves can be chased with the round-ended shallow gouge, which can also be used to stab them (Fig 15.14).

Acute Angles

When stabbing the centre lines of the oblique strokes of A, K, M, N, V, W, X and Y into a crumbly wood, great care must be taken not to cut right up to the inside of the angle as the wedge action of the chisel can dislodge the inner apex point when the second centre line is stabbed in (Fig 15.15). It is best to use a chisel which cuts from the top of the bottom serifs (in the A and M) but is only wide enough to reach the level of the inside apex (*see* Figs 15.8, 15.9). When the sides have been stabbed or chased for this distance the chisel can be stabbed in lightly to make the two centre-line cuts meet in the middle of the point. A third stab mark is made from this point to the outside tip of the letter, pressing the corner in where they meet and resting the edge up to the surface at the outside point. If a little is then pared off the sides from the inside of the apex towards the outside enough wood will have been removed to prevent the wedge action occurring. The remainder of each letter is then chased out with the skew chisel. When chasing at an angle other than parallel or perpendicular to the grain it is essential to stroke the fibres of the grain together to prevent splitting.

The Basic Straight Letter Stroke

Start practising with the letter I. Hold the straight-edged chisel vertically on the centre line (you have to get used to judging where this is), making sure that there is room for the inward slope of the serif at each end (*see* Fig 15.8). With a smart blow of the mallet drive it in a good way. A piece of tape bound round the blade at the right distance up from the edge of the chisel will tell how near you are to the correct depth of cut. Then rest the edge on one side of the letter at about 45° to the surface, and with another blow drive it to the bottom of the first cut (*see* Fig 15.9), and then do the same from the opposite side. It does not pay to miss your aim the first time then fiddle with it to correct it.

The Serif

For the serifs you will find a fishtail gouge of No. 3 or 4 sweep (English), or No. 3 (Swiss), most effective. Be particular in sharpening it so that its edge is straight from corner to corner (Figs 15.16–15.20).

Rest it flute down against one side of the V cut pointing towards the serif a little way back from the end of the cut. Engage its edge lightly with the wood and push it forward and round in to the corner of the serif. As it travels its lower corner should dig deeper. The angle of the tool's edge to the surface at the end of the cut should be 45°. The same cut is made on the opposite side. With the flute still facing down at 45°, place the corner of the chisel on one corner of the serif and drive it down to the middle of the serif. If it is then rocked up to meet the other corner a neat triangle of wood will chip out. Try to keep the end of the serif concave. This procedure is almost identical to that for creating triangular pockets described in Chapter 3.

FIG 15.15 *Practice alphabet in mahogany. Notice the missing inner apices of the M, N and W. This alphabet is inconsistent in the depths of some letters. The counters of P and R should not be the same size.*

FIG 15.16 *The first cut into the serif on an M.*

FIG 15.17 *The end of the stroke with the fishtail No. 3 tilted at 45°. The corner buried in the wood should be lower than the V cut along the stroke behind it.*

FIG 15.18 *The fishtail cutting the right foot serif.*

FIG 15.19 *The fishtail being used flute-down to start the end of the serif with a chip cut. This should produce a concave end to the serif.*

FIG 15.20 *The end of the chip cut with the edge of the gouge rocked into the opposite corner.*

FIG 15.21 *Chasing a flared side to a stem with a skew chisel.*

FIG 15.22 *The shape of the letter shown. The skew has to have a fairly blunt angle at its tip to reach into the corner of the serif. If it were more acute it would dig in and make a mess.*

CHASING STRAIGHT LETTERS

Letters chased with the skew chisel (Figs 15.21, 15.22) are like those in the drawn alphabet (*see* Fig 15.2) and have gently flaring sides. They take longer to carve but are more attractive.

S – Problems of Curves and Curves ending in Serifs

For carving an S, start by stabbing a short straight cut along the middle of the centre line. After stabbing the rest of the centre line with gouges which match the curves, stab in the ends of the serifs across the grain to prevent splitting when the trough is cut. This cut is made with the fishtail from one corner of the serif to the other, keeping it slanted at 45° as for the I. To shape the inside curves either stab down with an appropriate gouge or chase them in the same way as for the O, working always with the grain.

Cutting Horizontal Members

It is important to make stop cuts across the grain to prevent splitting and, after stabbing the centre lines, to chase the sides of the grooves, observing any slight slope in the grain (Figs 15.23–15.25).

The Tails of R and Q

With R and Q, carve the counter before cutting the tail. The tips of the tails can be chased or chip-carved with a shallow gouge.

TACKLING AN INSCRIPTION

It is sensible to practise all letters several times on spare pieces of wood before trying the real thing. When carving an inscription start with all the full-length vertical strokes. Stab every centre line and then the same slope on the side of every one. This ensures speed and consistency. I prefer to leave the serifs until all the main strokes are done. If the first letter is a difficult one, leave it until later. A mistake is more noticeable at the beginning and end. If there are several lines to tackle, cut the remaining letters from the bottom up. This reduces smudging of the drawing.

If the lettering is to be painted tests must be done to see if the paint will bleed along the grain. If it tends to do this the panel should be sealed with a clear varnish or sealer compatible with the paint. When the paint is dry the surface can be sanded to fresh wood. Sanding will probably be needed to clean the surface.

FIG 15.23 *The fishtail cutting the end of the serif on the arm of a T as a stop cut.*

FIG 15.24 *Stabbing the centre line of the arm of a T.*

Always sand along the grain, using the finest paper that works. The paper must be used wrapped around a firm rubbing block to prevent the blurring of the edges of the letters. If you take much off the surface the shapes of the letters will be different.

Lettering in wood is both useful and an art form. It is also an enormous benefit, whether or not you intend to make carving your profession, in what it teaches about design, about self-criticism and about physical control.

FIG 15.25 *Chasing the side of the arm of the T with a skew chisel.*

APPENDIX

A Personal List of Woods

B elow I list woods that I have used and, although I do not recommend all of them, you should nevertheless try a wide variety.

Using Exotic Timbers

There are innumerable exotic timbers available, although many of those that are found in builders merchants' yards are more suited to construction than to carving: they may be splintery or mushy or have interlocked grain. Some available timbers, particularly tropical ones, come from uncontrolled deforestation, and if our use of them encourages this practice we should avoid them. This deforestation harms the natural inhabitants of the forests and threatens the stability of life on this planet. I used tropical timbers before this became an issue, but I would not use them now unless they came from old buildings or furniture. In fact, you do not need to look abroad for unusual woods. There are many trees felled in this country that are burnt or left to rot because their owners or the fellers do not realize their value to woodworkers. Many exotics have been grown as ornamental trees and are blown down or felled for good reasons. Sizeable shrubs may also provide fascinating timber. If you keep your eyes open you can find sufficient quantity and variety to satisfy most needs.

Hardwoods

Acacia (*Robinia pseudacacia*) An ornamental tree. Fairly dense; works rather like oak; can be splintery. Yellow on first cutting; turns golden brown on exposure. Takes detail.

Afrormosia (*Pericopsis elata*) A brown, fibrous wood resembling iroko. Very durable. Splintery with interlocked grain. Acceptable for incised lettering but not recommended for detailed carving. Tropical.

Alder (*Alnus glutinosa*) Pale yellow or pinkish even-grained timber, tough and slightly woolly. Will take detail. Somewhat like lime.

Apple (*Malus spp.*) Dense, pink, even-grained heartwood. Tougher than pearwood. Takes detail. Can split badly when drying. Prone to woodworm attack when damp.

Arbutus (*Arbutus unedo*) An ornamental tree. Very hard, pink timber, requiring strength and persistence. Little figure. Can split badly when drying. Takes detail.

Ash (*Fraxinus excelsior*) Attractive white or pinkish ring-porous wood. Easier to carve when slow grown (more than 10 rings to 25mm [1in]). Renowned for toughness. Carves easily when green. Not suitable for fine detail. Sometimes has brown, streaky figure in heart (olive ash). Of the same family as the olive tree.

Balsa (*Ochroma pyramidale*) The lightest commercial timber. White or pinkish. Very soft, requiring the sharpest of chisels. Best avoided except for carving model aeroplanes.

Basswood (*Tilia americana*) The American form of the lime tree. Similar working properties to European lime.

Beech (*Fagus sylvatica*) A white, very tough, even-grained wood. When steamed is pinkish and more cheesy to cut. Excellent for letter cutting. Will take detail but requires great effort and patience for carving unless cut green. Prone to beetle attack and rot while seasoning.

Birch (*Betula spp.*) A whitish, close-grained, even-textured wood much carved in Scandinavia. Pleasantly lustrous. Denser than lime and inclined to break short. Very difficult to season without mould staining or rot.

Blackwood (African blackwood) (*Dalbergia melanoxylon*) Very black and one of the hardest woods there is. Chisels need to have thicker edges than normal. Easier to work with rasps.

Box (*Buxus sempervirens*) Beautiful, very dense, yellowish wood. Available only in small sizes. Takes extremely fine detail.

Broom (*Genista aetnensis*) A pale-brown, dense, hard wood. Slightly stringy but takes fine detail. Distinctive axial parenchyma pattern similar to that in acacia and other leguminous trees visible on end grain. Available only in small sizes.

Catalpa (Indian Bean Tree) (*Catalpa bignonioides*) An ornamental tree that can have a wide trunk. Pale-brown, lightweight, ring-porous wood. Carves very easily. Seasons very quickly. Distinctive smell. Can take fine detail but inclined to be stringy. May be mistaken for elm or ash.

Cherry (*Prunus avium*) A hard, dense, pale-yellow, brown or orangey-coloured semi-ring-porous wood with noticeable figure. Pale sapwood that splits badly in drying. Heartwood also hard to season. Takes fine detail.

Chestnut (horse chestnut) (*Aesculus hippocastanum*) A very pale, beautifully, lustrous timber with even texture but prone to have spiral grain, ripple figure and large areas of silica deposits. Can be carved with care but tends to break off short like birch.

Chestnut (sweet chestnut) (*Castanea sativa*) A pale, fairly light, ring-porous wood sometimes mistaken for oak but with inconspicuous rays. Durable and stable. Carves beautifully. Can take fine detail but earlywood inclined to crumble.

Cotoneaster (*Cotoneaster watereri*) An ornamental shrub or small tree. Wood is orangey-brown, dense and even-textured. Hard. Takes detail.

Ebony (*Diospyros ebenum*) Largely black but may have pink streaks in heartwood. Very dense and hard, even-textured wood. Beautiful appearance but needs steep bevels on chisels or to be worked with rasps. Wear goggles when carving with mallet and chisel. Tropical.

Elder (*Sambucus nigra*) A pale, yellowy-green, dense, even-textured timber with tendency to spiral grain. Large pith. Small sizes only. More desirable as a curiosity than to be recommended for carving.

Elm (*Ulmus spp.*) A pale, greyish-brown, ring-porous timber with noticeable figure. Sometimes has interlocked grain. May be exceptionally tough and hard but may carve more easily than oak. Inclined to crumble.

Hawthorn (*Crataegus oxyacantha*) A common small tree inclined to spiral growth and other deformities. Wood may be pink, brown or orange, or a mixture. Very dense. Usually in small sizes. Inclined to split badly when drying.

Holly (*Ilex aquifolium*) Very dense, bone-white wood of even texture and good lustre. Rots easily and is difficult to season without mould staining. Splits badly during drying. If, with luck, it does not split and keeps white it is beautiful but very hard. Takes fine detail.

Hornbeam (*Carpinus betulus*) A pale, yellowish-white, close-grained, even-textured wood. Slightly stringy and tough. Resents being carved against the grain. Rather like holly but not as hard.

Imbuia (Brazilian walnut) (*Phoebe porosa*) Yellow on first exposure, darkening to reddish brown. Strongly figured. Aromatic on first being cut. Carves easily but may have curly grain. A tropical timber.

Iroko (*Chlorophora excelsa*) Apart from being yellow when first cut is very like afrormosia in appearance and suitability for carving. Very durable. Tropical.

Jelutong (*Dyera costulata*) A lustrous pale-yellow, close-grained, even-textured, lightweight wood. Very stable. Carves very easily but sharp edges and other fine details crumble easily. Absence of figure suits it for lamination. Oval slots are remnants of latex canals and may need to be plugged. Tropical, but probably from managed forest.

Khaya (African mahogany) (*Khaya ivorensis*) A pink wood, less crisp and dense than true mahogany. Tends to have interlocked grain. Can take detail if carved carefully but may crumble on sharp edges. Tropical.

Laburnum (*Laburnum anagyroides*) A small ornamental tree. Very dense ring-porous wood with strong figure. Yellowish-green on first being cut, darkening to chocolate brown. Very pale sapwood. Very slow drying and likely to have light fungal patches in heartwood. Juvenile wood around heart often has long shakes in it. Very hard. Takes fine detail. Typical axial parenchyma patterns on end grain common to other leguminous trees, e.g. acacia and broom.

Lauan (Philippines mahogany) (*Shorea spp.*) Various timbers, ranging from pink to yellow, of varying hardness and toughness. Hard varieties can be carved but have interlocked grain and can be stringy. Tropical.

Lignum vitae (*Guaiacum officinale and G. sanctum*) Very heavy, dense, brown or greenish-blue and yellow timber with yellow sapwood. Very interlocked grain. Very hard. Can be carved but eye protection should be worn. Chisel bevels need to be steep. Tropical.

Lime (*Tilia vulgaris*) White, creamy or pinkish, close-grained, even-textured fairly lightweight wood. Exceptionally easy to carve. Takes fine detail. Will tolerate being carved against the grain. Bland figure makes it suitable for lamination. Has no lustre. Not usually attractive for large, simple forms.

Magnolia (*Magnolia spp.*) Small ornamental trees and shrubs in Britain. Pale, greenish-yellow, close-grained, even-textured wood. Similar working properties to lime but more attractive because of lustre.

Mahogany (*Swietenia macrophylla*) Various types ranging in density from medium to hard. Colour varies with hardness from pink to deep reddish-brown. Darker kinds have good figure. Tends to have interlocked grain. Inclined to be brittle and to crumble on sharp edges on short grain, but can take detail with care. Tropical.

Maple (field maple) (*Acer campestre*) Dense white or pinkish timber. Resembles sycamore. Very hard when seasoned but carves well when green. Decays easily. May have dark patches of silica deposits. Takes fine detail.

Mulberry (*Morus alba and M. nigra*) Bright yellow when freshly cut. Darkens to reddish-yellow colour. Ring-porous timber with simple figure. Carves very easily.

Oak (Holm oak) (*Quercus ilex*) Dense, hard wood. Pale brown with strong ray patterns. Very like white oak in appearance but harder to cut. Takes detail.

Oak (White/European oak) (*Quercus petraea and Q. robur*) Colour varies from fawn to dark brown. Ring-porous wood; much easier to work when slow grown. Even figure and large rays. Not as difficult to carve as some people think. Can take fine detail. Sharp edges may crumble. Durable.

Oak (Red/American oak) (*Quercus rubra*) A redder brown than white oak. Wood more open-grained and stringy but can carve easily and take detail. Inclined to crumble.

Obeche (*Triplochiton swietenia*) An open-grained, pale-yellow or white wood; soft and crumbly with interlocked grain. Carves easily with sharp tools but uninteresting to look at. Difficult to finish cleanly. Can be used for maquettes. Tropical.

Padauk (padouk) (*Pterocarpus spp.*) The Malaysian variety is a startling orange-red on first being cut. It dulls to a purplish brown. The African type is more brown. It is a hard, large-pored, splintery wood with interlocked grain. Not easy to carve or finish with the chisel. Tropical.

Pear (*Pyrus communis*) A dense, fine-textured, even-grained timber. Mature heartwood an even pink colour, occasionally with brown streaks. Sapwood and immature heart look very like cherry. Like cherry, seasons very slowly; can split badly – possibly best if bark is left on but will need watching for beetle attack. A hard wood but crisp and able to take very fine detail.

Plane (*Platanus hybrida*) A white or pale-brown wood, sometimes mistaken for beech. Radially sawn boards are sold as 'lacewood' because of the beautiful ray figure. Can split badly when drying but large pieces are possible. An easy wood to carve, almost as soft as lime. Detailed work may be camouflaged by the ray figure.

Plum (*Prunus communis*) A dense, fine-textured, even-grained timber with yellow, orange, pink, purple or brown patches. Much spiral grain. Is seasoned with great difficulty – splits frequently. Perhaps seasoned best with bark on or sawn or cleft into quarters or boards.

Poplar (*Populus spp.*) A grey-white timber, sometimes reddish. Even-grained, fine-textured but light wood. Used for carving in Italy but rather woolly and more spongy than lime. Will take detail but requires very sharp chisels. Prone to rot and beetle attack unless carefully seasoned.

Rhododendron (*Rhododendron spp.*) A small ornamental tree or shrub. Dense, attractive, fine-grained yellowish timber. Liable to have ripple figure. Can be carved into fine detail but inclined to break off short.

Rosewood (*Dalbergia spp.*) A number of different tropical timbers including tulipwood, Brazilian rosewood and Indian rosewood. Use them if your conscience permits. Colours may be dark chocolate brown with yellow streaks (Brazilian), yellowish with pink streaks (tulipwood) and pink with dark streaks (Indian). Varying texture from coarse to fine. Splintery and hard.

Rowan (mountain ash) (*Sorbus aucuparia*) Pale grey-brown, with fine even-textured grain. Little figure. Fairly tough but pleasant to carve. Can take detail.

Sapele (*Entandrophragma cylindricum*) Fairly dark reddish brown, can be mistaken for mahogany. Interlocked grain. A tropical timber. If it has to be used is more suitable for panelling or flooring.

Satinwood (Ceylon) (*Chloroxylon swietenia*) A dense, yellow wood with fiercely interlocked grain. Very splintery. Beautiful stripey figure. Very lustrous. Difficult to carve but rewarding – needs final sanding. Tropical, and therefore must be sanctioned by your conscience.

Sumach (*Rhus typhina*) A small ornamental tree. Soft, yellowish-green and brown ring-porous wood. Coarse-textured. Strong figure; has large pith in centre. Only in small dimensions. White sapwood prone to beetle attack. Not good for detail. An interesting curiosity.

Sycamore (*Acer pseudoplatanus*) A pale creamy-white, fine-textured and even-grained tough timber. Little figure. Good lustre. When green carves easily. Hard when dry. Toughness makes it difficult to carve without leaving whiskers. Can take fine detail. Prone to mould stain and beetle attack. Rots quickly if not stored properly.

Teak (*Tectona grandis*) An oily, dark yellowish-brown, coarse-grained timber. Carves easily but quickly dulls the edges of tools. Attractive figure. Occasionally has interlocked grain. Tends to crumble on sharp edges. Very durable. Tropical.

Tulip tree (*Liriodendron tulipifera*) One of the magnolias. Grown as an ornamental. Can be large. Pale greenish-yellow, fine-textured, even-grained timber of medium density. Carves like lime. May have pink or mauve streaks. Good lustre. Needs care in seasoning as rots easily, and is susceptible to woodworm.

Utile (*Entandrophragma utile*) A fairly coarse-textured, reddish-brown timber. Interlocked splintery grain. Difficult to carve but handsome, very like sapele but coarser. Resembles mahogany. Durable heartwood. Tropical.

Walnut (European walnut) (*Juglans regia*) Greyish brown with hints of purple, strongly figured heartwood. Sapwood pale brown. Looks coarse-grained but carves well and takes fine detail. Fairly tough. Very handsome. Very rich dark brown when finished with linseed oil. Sapwood prone to crumble when carved. Moderately durable.

Walnut (American or black walnut) (*Juglans nigra*) Similar to *Juglans regia* but more purple in colour. Grain and figure more regular. Carves easily and takes fine detail. Very durable.

SOFTWOODS

Cedar of Lebanon (*Cedrus Libani*) Strongly figured golden or pale pinkish-brown wood. Brittle and soft, but can carve well and look beautiful. Very strongly aromatic – deterrent to insects.

Cypress (*Cupressus spp.*) The sapwood is best avoided as it is cotton-woolly. Heartwood is firm, pale creamy pink, and carves rather like lime. May have many knots.

Fir (*Picea abies*) A whitish wood very like pine. Slow-grown wood with 20 or more rings to the

25mm (1in) is best, but inclined to be mushy and have many knots. Not recommended.

Gingko (maidenhair tree) (*Gingko biloba*) A comparatively uncommon ornamental tree. A dense, even-textured, pale-yellow wood. Lightweight but hard. Will take detail.

Larch (*Larix decidua*) Rich reddish-brown, open-grained timber. Not suitable for detailed work. Many knots. Splits while seasoning. Harder than pine. Moderately durable.

Pine (parana pine) (*Araucaria brasiliana*) An even-textured, fine-grained, golden-brown wood with pink and lighter yellow or brown areas. Denser than most pines, with a slight spongy feel when carved. Can take detail but is hard work. Best kept for high-grade joinery.

Pine (pitch pine) (*Pinus palustris*) A very resinous, dense, coarse-grained, reddish-gold wood. Strong demarcation between earlywood and latewood. Carves like cheese when green but dries to be very hard with much splitting. Hard work but handsome if carved successfully. Can take fine detail.

Pine (Scots pine) (*Pinus sylvestris*) Sometimes sold as European redwood. Modern trees are grown fast and seldom to full maturity, so are mostly sapwood. The earlywood of fast-grown pine is abundant and very crumbly when carved across the grain. Earlywood is white, latewood is orange. Heartwood of old, slow-grown timber is more pink or orange with a more even texture, and can be carved easily with fine detail. Look for wood with at least 20 rings to 25mm (1in).

Pine (yellow pine) (*Pinus strobus*) The kind to ask for is Quebec yellow pine. Southern yellow pine is much coarser in texture with large expanses of easily torn earlywood. Quebec yellow pine is a lightweight, light-yellow or pink even-grained timber with gradual transition from latewood to earlywood. A delight to carve with sharp chisels. Takes fine detail. Splinters and tears easily.

Spruce (whitewood or white deal) (*Abies alba*) Lustrous pale yellowish-brown, fine-grained, even-textured soft wood. Slow-grown timber is carvable.

Yew (*Taxus baccata*) A beautiful pink, orange or reddish-gold, fine-grained heartwood. Sapwood startlingly white. Gradual transition from latewood to earlywood. Splinters easily and can run away from the chisel following undulations in the grain. Can take detail. Needs great care in carving, especially in finishing with chisels. Turns a beautiful red-gold with linseed oil.

FURTHER READING

E. M. Catich, *The Origin of The Serif* (Davenport, Iowa, 1991)

L. C. Evetts, *Roman Lettering* (Pitman and Sons, 1938)

Richard Grasby, *Lettercutting in Stone* (Anthony Nelson, 1989, and University of Pennsylvania Press)

Mary Duke Guldan, *A Woodcarver's Workbook* (Fox Chapel, second edition 1992)

Paul N. Hasluck, *A Manual of Traditional Woodcarving* (Dover, 1977)

Charles Hayward and William Wheeler, *Practical Woodcarving and Gilding* (Evans Bros, second edition 1973)

R. Bruce Hoadley, *Understanding Wood* (Taunton Press, 1980)

Chris Pye, *Woodcarving Tools, Materials and Equipment* (GMC Publications, 1994)

ABOUT THE AUTHOR

Dick Onians, born in 1940 in a house full of books, folk carvings and other sculpture, spent his childhood climbing trees, reading and whittling. He read Classics and English at Cambridge, took his PGCE at London University and taught English and Latin at Dudley Boys' Grammar School for three years. He then studied Woodcarving at The City and Guilds of London Art School under the late William Wheeler. From 1968 he taught English and sculpture part-time while establishing himself as a sculptor in wood and stone. In 1978 he returned to the City and Guilds Art School to teach part-time on its unique courses in traditional wood and stone carving. He is now the Senior Woodcarving Tutor there. In 1992 he pioneered the formal part-time Creative Studies course in woodcarving for the City and Guilds Institute, which he teaches at Missenden Abbey, Buckinghamshire.

He also teaches at many other colleges near his home in Hertfordshire and around the country. He is a regular contributor to *Woodcarving* magazine and is an associate of the Royal Society of British Sculptors. Although versatile as a sculptor he prefers to carve his own abstract shapes in wood and stone. He has exhibited widely in one-man and group exhibitions, and his work is in private collections around the world.

INDEX

TITLES AVAILABLE FROM
GMC Publications

BOOKS

WOODWORKING

40 More Woodworking Plans & Projects	*GMC Publications*	Making Chairs and Tables	*GMC Publications*
Bird Boxes & Feeders for the Garden	*Dave Mackenzie*	Making Unusual Miniatures	*Graham Spalding*
Complete Woodfinishing	*Ian Hosker*	Pine Furniture Projects	*Dave Mackenzie*
Electric Woodwork	*Jeremy Broun*	Security for the Householder:	
Furniture Projects	*Rod Wales*	Fitting Locks & Other Devices	*E. Phillips*
Furniture Restoration (Practical Crafts)	*Kevin Jan Bonner*	Sharpening Pocket Reference Book	*Jim Kingshott*
Furniture Restoration for Beginners	*Kevin Jan Bonner*	Sharpening: The Complete Guide	*Jim Kingshott*
Green Woodwork	*Mike Abbott*	The Incredible Router	*Jeremy Broun*
Making & Modifying Woodworking Tools	*Jim Kingshott*	The Workshop	*Jim Kingshott*
Making Fine Furniture	*Tom Darby*	Tool Making for Woodworkers	*Ray Larsen*
Making Little Boxes from Wood	*John Bennett*	Woodfinishing Handbook (Practical Crafts)	*Ian Hosker*
Making Shaker Furniture	*Barry Jackson*	Woodworking Plans & Projects	*GMC Publications*

WOODTURNING

Adventures in Woodturning	*David Springett*	Practical Tips for Turners & Carvers	*GMC Publications*
Bert Marsh: Woodturner	*Bert Marsh*	Practical Tips for Woodturners	*GMC Publications*
Bill Jones' Notes from the Turning Shop	*Bill Jones*	Spindle Turning	*GMC Publications*
Bill Jones' Further Notes from the Turning Shop	*Bill Jones*	Turning Miniatures in Wood	*John Sainsbury*
Colouring Techniques for Woodturners	*Jan Sanders*	Turning Wooden Toys	*Terry Lawrence*
Decorative Techniques for Woodturners	*Hilary Bowen*	Understanding Woodturning	*Ann & Bob Phillips*
Essential Tips for Woodturners	*GMC Publications*	Useful Woodturning Projects	*GMC Publications*
Faceplate Turning	*GMC Publications*	Woodturning Jewellery	*Hilary Bowen*
Fun at the Lathe	*R.C. Bell*	Woodturning Masterclass	*Tony Boase*
Illustrated Woodturning Techniques	*John Hunnex*	Woodturning Projects	*GMC Publications*
Keith Rowley's Woodturning Projects	*Keith Rowley*	Woodturning Techniques	*GMC Publications*
Make Money from Woodturning	*Ann & Bob Phillips*	Woodturning Wizardry	*David Springett*
Multi-Centre Woodturning	*Ray Hopper*	Woodturning: A Foundation Course	*Keith Rowley*
Pleasure and Profit from Woodturning	*Reg Sherwin*	Woodturning: A Sourcebook of Shapes	*John Hunnex*

WOODCARVING

Carving Birds & Beasts	*GMC Publications*	The Woodcarvers	*GMC Publications*
Carving on Turning	*Chris Pye*	Understanding Woodcarving	*GMC Publications*
Carving Realistic Birds	*David Tippey*	Wildfowl Carving - Volume 1	*Jim Pearce*
Decorative Woodcarving	*Jeremy Williams*	Wildfowl Carving - Volume 2	*Jim Pearce*
Essential Tips for Woodcarvers	*GMC Publications*	Woodcarving for Beginners	*GMC Publications*
Essential Woodcarving Techniques	*Dick Onians*	Woodcarving Tools, Materials & Equipment	*Chris Pye*
Lettercarving in Wood	*Chris Pye*	Woodcarving: A Complete Course	*Ron Butterfield*
The Art of the Woodcarver	*GMC Publications*	Woodcarving: A Foundation Course	*Zoë Gertner*

UPHOLSTERY

Seat Weaving (Practical Crafts)	*Ricky Holdstock*	Upholstery Techniques & Projects	*David James*
Upholsterer's Pocket Reference Book	*David James*	Upholstery: A Complete Course	*David James*
Upholstery Restoration Projects	*David James*		

TOYMAKING

Designing & Making Wooden Toys	*Terry Kelly*	Making Wooden Toys & Games	*Jeff & Jennie Loader*
Fun to Make Wooden Toys & Games	*Jeff & Jennie Loader*	Restoring Rocking Horses	*Clive Green & Anthony Dew*
Making Board, Peg & Dice Games	*Jeff & Jennie Loader*		

DOLLS' HOUSES

Architecture for Dolls' Houses	*Joyce Percival*	Making Period Dolls' House Accessories	*Andrea Barham*
Beginners' Guide to the Dolls' House Hobby	*Jean Nisbett*	Making Period Dolls' House Furniture	*Derek & Sheila Rowbottom*
Dolls' House Bathrooms: Lots of Little Loos	*Patricia King*	Making Tudor Dolls' Houses	*Derek & Sheila Rowbottom*
Easy to Make Dolls' House Accessories	*Andrea Barham*	Making Victorian Dolls' House Furniture	*Patricia King*
Make Your Own Dolls' House Furniture	*Maurice Harper*	Miniature Needlepoint Carpets	*Janet Granger*
Making Dolls' House Furniture	*Patricia King*	The Complete Dolls' House Book	*Jean Nisbett*
Making Georgian Dolls' Houses	*Derek & Sheila Rowbottom*	The Secrets of the Dolls' House Makers	*Jean Nisbett*

CRAFTS

Celtic Knotwork Designs	*Sheila Sturrock*	Embroidery Tips & Hints	*Harold Hayes*
Collage from Seeds, Leaves and Flowers	*Joan Carver*	Making Knitwear Fit	*Pat Ashforth & Steve Plummer*
Complete Pyrography	*Stephen Poole*	Pyrography Handbook (Practical Crafts)	*Stephen Poole*
Creating Knitwear Designs	*Pat Ashforth & Steve Plummer*	Tassel Making for Beginners	*Enid Taylor*
Cross Stitch Kitchen Projects	*Janet Granger*	Tatting Collage	*Lindsay Rogers*
Cross Stitch on Colour	*Sheena Rogers*		

VIDEOS

Drop-in and Pinstuffed Seats	*David James*	Classic Profiles	*Dennis White*
Stuffover Upholstery	*David James*	Twists and Advanced Turning	*Dennis White*
Elliptical Turning	*David Springett*	Sharpening the Professional Way	*Jim Kingshott*
Woodturning Wizardry	*David Springett*	Sharpening Turning & Carving Tools	*Jim Kingshott*
Turning Between Centres	*Dennis White*	Bowl Turning	*John Jordan*
Turning Bowls	*Dennis White*	Hollow Turning	*John Jordan*
Boxes, Goblets & Screw Threads	*Dennis White*	Woodturning: A Foundation Course	*Keith Rowley*
Novelties and Projects	*Dennis White*	Carving a Figure - The Female Form	*Ray Gonzalez*

MAGAZINES

WOODTURNING ◆ WOODCARVING ◆ TOYMAKING
FURNITURE & CABINETMAKING ◆ BUSINESSMATTERS
CREATIVE IDEAS FOR THE HOME ◆ THE ROUTER

————————— ◆ —————————

The above represents a full list of all titles currently published or scheduled to be published. All are available direct from the Publishers or through bookshops, newsagents and specialist retailers. To place an order, or to obtain a complete catalogue, contact:

GMC Publications,
166 High Street, Lewes, East Sussex BN7 1XU United Kingdom
Tel: 01273 488005 Fax: 01273 478606

Orders by credit card are accepted